LRC

Learning Resource Centre

Barcode: 154913

To renew your loans:

Call: 01227 81 11 66
Email: lrc@eastkentcollege.ac.uk
Online: tiny.cc/renew-my-books

Please see below for the date your book is due back

GOD HAS NOT CHANGED

Alice Thomas Ellis

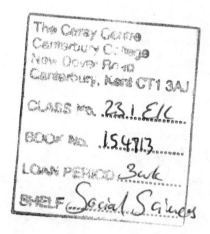
burns & oates

Burns & Oates is a Continuum imprint

Continuum
The Tower Building   15 East 26th Street
11 York Road   New York
London SE1 7NX   NY 10010

www.continuumbooks.com

Published in association with *The Oldie*
Articles © Alice Thomas Ellis 2004
Introduction © Richard Ingrams 2004

First published 2004

British Library Cataloguing-in-Publication Data
A catalogue record for this book is available from the British Library.

ISBN 0-86012-359-6

Designed and typeset by Benn Linfield
Printed and bound by Cromwell Press, Trowbridge, Wiltshire

CONTENTS

CONTENTS

CONTENTS

INTRODUCTION

'Readers have got to be annoyed' – Lord Beaverbrook's maxim is reassurance to editors like myself when the angry letters flood in. But the editor of the *Universe*, for which Alice Thomas Ellis used to write a weekly column, did not share the same view. In 1994 she was sacked, at the insistence of the English Catholic Bishop.

The *Universe*'s loss was the *Oldie*'s gain and she has been writing a regular monthly column for me ever since, joining a band of misfits and drop-outs for whom I have provided a soap-box from which to air their views. Whilst not necessarily agreeing with all their opinions I admire their general outspokenness and their ability, not always easy to explain, to annoy the readers.

Apart from the *Universe*, Alice Thomas Ellis managed to upset various sections of the Catholic hierarchy by refusing to go along with the changes that she saw taking place in the church. This was not just a question of liturgy or church furnishings – though both have come in for their fair share of attacks from her pen – it was more to do with a general tendency common to all churches in modern times of wanting to be all things to all men, and especially to all women (in other words, not to upset the feminists). The outward and visible signs of the change were the carpet in the aisle and the smiling face that was to be seen on the faces of the priesthood and the laity, the message being that religion makes you happy and that whatever happens, Jesus loves you.

Alice is here to remind us that life isn't like that. Religion, and Christianity in particular, involves difficulties and doubt. But that is only because it confronts the realities of life. The modern tendency which you can witness most mornings on the BBC's *Thought for the Day* is that the listeners are having a good time. It is rather like the way people on all sides, whether in shops or on trains, say Have a nice day, rudely and insensitively ignoring the obvious fact that many people know in advance that the one thing they are not going to have is a nice day – they could be going into hospital for a painful operation, visiting a dying relative or coping with an attack of depression brought on by a marriage break-up. Quite apart from the everyday worries common to all.

Whether in person or in writing Alice does not present a smiling face. I can see her with her large soulful eyes standing by the kitchen stove in her house, now, alas, sold, in Gloucester Crescent NW1 listening to the conversation, puffing on a fag, reminding me always of Stevie Smith's observation – 'Holy people do not usually feel at all at home; one always thinks of them as awkward, with a look coming out of their eyes to say they wish they were elsewhere.'

The mistake would be to imagine that Alice is an unworldly, reclusive character pining to be in the convent she joined but was forced to leave because of ill-health. She is the writer of a batch of short, sharp novels, and in her capacity as publisher along with her late husband Colin Haycraft has acted as a mid-wife to a number of aspiring novelists and contributed a long-running Home Life column to the *Spectator*. She has somehow managed, at the same time, to mother seven children and later to look after several grandchildren as well. All this in addition to being an exceptional cook.

When therefore she writes about religion she does so not from the point of view of an unworldly mystic but that of a woman who has had her fair share of practical experience, not to mention suffering and tragedy. This gives all her reflections a special strength, as they cannot be dismissed as those of some-one who has retreated from life. Here is a woman who has seen it all, been there, done that and come through with flying colours.

Traditionalist, conservative – these are now rude words. But in the context of religion it is harder to make them stick. God has not changed, any more than humans. The attempt by the churches – both Catholic and Protestant – to embrace modern ideas about psychology, feminism, sex or racial prejudice has led, as Alice warned her readers, not to an increase but a falling away of congregations. In this respect the churches are little different from various other institutions one can think of – the BBC, the broadsheet newspapers – which have tried to widen their appeal and in particular to attract the young, and only succeeded in dumbing down, and falling between several stools; in the process losing, not gaining an audience.

Is there a gloomy, carping, I-told-you-so note to Alice's reflections? Not a bit of it. Like most people of an essentially pessimistic frame of mind, she is unfailingly cheerful and amusing, in marked contrast to some of her critics who include, I regret to say, many prominent members of the Catholic intelligentsia.

As for her readers, my feeling is that people who read about religion, even the non-believers, prefer a good strong, old-fashioned brew to the watered down draught on offer from the *Thought for the Day* merchants. They may get annoyed, as Lord Beaverbrook wanted, but I suspect they quite enjoy the aggravation.

Richard Ingrams

1. 'WIMMIN'

I recently asked a young – well youngish – friend (forty-two to be exact) what she thought of feminists. 'Hate them,' she responded tersely. She is an editor on a New York magazine, elegant, witty, confident and acknowledging no debt to the Sisters. She reminds me very much of certain film stars of the 30s and 40s – Katherine Hepburn, Joan Crawford, Bette Davis, etc., none of whom resemble in the least the downtrodden wimps so crucial to feminist myth. Modern Woman was coming along nicely until after the war, when Baby Doll emerged – Lord knows where from – to be counterbalanced by the Amazon who, even if she did not slice off a breast, burned her bra (which, when you come to consider it, was foolish, since if you are going in for drawing bows a little structural support in the background can only be beneficial). Disgruntled females organized 'consciousness raising sessions' and adopted other outmoded and discredited Marxist tactics, so that in a while everyone hated them, though few dared to admit it. A dreadful breed of feminist men arose, claiming to sympathize with this struggle for justice, and everyone hated them too.

Social engineering is not a good idea. Human nature just will not have it. In LA a few years ago I sat with a group of ladies round a lunch table. They wore the baffled and aggrieved expression of hyenas who cannot understand why their prey is proving elusive. They all had jobs but no men and they could not imagine why this should be so. They had done all the right things – loved and esteemed themselves highly, explained to men what chauvinist pigs they were, been to assertiveness classes and thought hard before shaving their legs. Those with an ex-husband demanded that he support them, for the rest of their lives, no matter what the relative state of their salaries, and then wondered despairingly why most men appeared to be homosexual. They were unaware of the extent of their unattractiveness: their greed, their humourlessness, their whingeing, their lack of generosity and the unsightly cut of their jackets.

Many of them still give the impression of being mad. A group recently carted round a church crucifix with a female on it – happily not a real one – referring to the curious thing as Jesa Crista. Sheer, pure nuttiness can go no further. Never mind that it's blasphemous, it is silly to suggest that historical figures can change sex. Was General Custer a girl? Mussolini a madam? The recorded circumcision of Our Lord was used as evidence against the early heresies as proof of his humanity. It must surely also serve as evidence of his maleness.

I have another question I should like answered. What if God had chosen to send a daughter to redeem us? What would the feminists say to that? You can bet your boots – and your hat and coat and gloves – that they'd be whining that women had to do everything: men were just absolutely hopeless and never did anything useful. Here was this poor woman suffering unspeakable agonies for us and what were the men doing, eh? One 'feminist theologian' (sic) I spoke to gave it as her opinion that if Our Lord couldn't be represented as female then females couldn't be sure that they were redeemed. I know people are thick but surely they can't be as thick as that. As long as equality is construed as meaning 'identical' we are going down skidding on good intentions to the inky bottom. The Cardinal, a well-meaning soul, has just said something about the Church 'going forward' – an unfortunate concept to apply to an edifice built upon a rock. If it starts padding in all directions after whatever fad or fancy is presently beguiling the 'intellectuals', it will collapse into nothing more than a pizza parlour (a nightmare predicted in the light of newly-built churches) and everyone can choke on their chosen flavour.

2. ALMOND ESSENCE

Amongst my correspondence of the past few weeks there were two contrasting letters – one from a supermarket and one from the Papal Nuncio. Both were responses to pained enquiry. In the first case we had bought two cream cakes, borne them home, immediately opened the packet which housed them and fallen back aghast, for a strong aroma of what I suspected might be cyanide wafted out. It was possible that someone had merely been lavish with the almond essence, but the smell was too overpowering to be ignored. We returned them to the store and waited for an explanation.

In the second case I had been wondering why, when the Church was so obviously in schism, nobody would admit it. I wrote in a spirit of honest enquiry to the above-mentioned person, asking what was going on, for God's sake.

To give him his due he did write back (mostly they don't), but he seemed rather to have missed the point, assuring me blandly that there was really nothing wrong at all. He had been all over the place in the last ten years, had the impression the Church was thriving and that hierarchy, priests and people shared a common sense of mission and devotion to the Holy See.

I had to sit down. Mass attendance is at what I believe is known as 'an all-time low', in many parishes the priest and people share nothing but misunderstanding and a cordial, mutual loathing (precise details on demand), and disobedience to the dictates of Rome is epidemic (again precise details on demand). I've described them frequently and am sick of repeating myself. If anyone is interested they might read *Serpent on the Rock* – a book I wrote on the subject. Also Fr Clifton's *The Alliance of Dissent*. There are many others – details on demand.

The Nuncio's letter ends with the breathtaking words, 'If the Church is to proclaim the truth in a credible fashion then it must present a unified aspect. That which damages this unity damages the proclamation of truth.'

Here I had to lie down. Of what truth does he speak? Is the

Blessed Sacrament the Body and Blood of Christ or not? Is the Virgin Birth fact or myth? Are the Commandments binding or only guidelines? Is there a God? There are many priests and teachers cheerfully expounding their own views on these interesting questions and what they say has no more relevance to Catholic doctrine than festering cream cakes. The letter was short as well as fatuous.

Now the one from the supermarket was an altogether different matter. It was long. It was implicit with profound feeling, with compassion and anxiety for our welfare. 'I was very concerned to learn of your dissatisfaction with two dairy cream strawberry slices purchased from our store.' It assures me in what I believe to be perfect truth that complaints such as mine are very rare. It proffers 'sincere apologies for any concern and inconvenience caused' and it adds, 'may I say how grateful we are to you for giving us the opportunity of further investigation and report.' Then it disgorges four quid in gift vouchers (they had already refunded the purchase price), which it 'hopes I will accept as a gesture of our appreciation for the time and trouble you have taken to bring this matter to our attention', and then it concludes by trusting that the store might continue to enjoy the pleasure of my much-valued custom.

You can say what you like about Mammon but when it comes to PR he leaves the Church standing – or rather, to be strictly accurate, floundering.

3. CHICKEN'S CHARTER

୧୬⟨⟩୬

I was reading an egg box the other day and discovered this Chicken's Charter: 'These eggs have been laid by hens that are provided with sufficient space indoors and out, in accordance with the strict standards laid out in the RSPCA's Freedom Food scheme. This scheme is monitored by the RSPCA and aims to ensure that the hens have the following five basic freedoms:

Freedom from Fear and Distress

Freedom from Pain, Injury or Disease

Freedom from Hunger and Thirst

Freedom from Discomfort

Freedom to express normal behaviour

'The range is actively managed to maintain the correct level of vegetation and to ensure hens are enclosed and protected from predators. For shelter and security at night, or in bad weather, the hens have housing with plenty of bedding and perch space, room to dust-bathe, preen and stretch their wings and quiet nest boxes in which to lay their eggs.'

Well, lucky old them, I thought. It had never previously occurred to me to envy a chicken. Such lives they lead. No problems. Can it, I wondered, be good for their characters? Should they not be stretched, at least to some degree, by the experience of misfortune, of sorrow and loss? Will they not grow up smug in their security and indifferent to the sufferings of their less fortunate kindred? Still, I don't suppose it matters much as long as they go on churning out the eggs.

But what, one asks oneself, will be their final fate? Will they be permitted to drop peacefully off the perch or does something more sinister await them? Will they end up swathed in clingfilm, exposed on the supermarket shelves like souls in Purgatory? I have to confess I don't know whether hens who have dedicated their lives to egg production are eventually destined for consumption, or whether they are pulped up as food for other hens, or whether they are buried with full ritual, as you might imagine, considering their privileged lifestyle.

Thinking about this, the thoughts turn with mysterious inevitability to the Archbishop of Canterbury. The other day he said we should be taught the difference between right and wrong. This was brave of him in the current climate of opinion, which differs in little, except for a few details, from the above charter, in its view of what is due to humanity. All rights and no duty. (Except in the case of hens laying a lot of eggs.)

He let himself down by failing to criticize the younger royals for their behaviour, but bravery has its limits. Chickens are no saints either and nobody blames them. I can feel myself going mad. It's all this New Age 'thought' which has crept into everything. While I'm quite prepared to believe that hens do not harbour Original Sin and are therefore entitled to a life free of worry, I cannot accept the same of humankind.

I cannot see why certain people believe only in 'original blessing' and are convinced that we have all developed to a state of near perfection and are as gods. Who? Where? How? What's the evidence? One of the foremost exponents of this proposition is one Matthew Fox, an ex-Dominican who now runs an institute of 'creation spirituality' in California and assures us we can do more or less as we like and need have no fear. He appears sillier than any old boiler but has a large following. His heresies present a danger to people's immortal souls and when I think of what foxes do in hen coops, I go quite cold.

4. COFFEE AND WINE

Over the course of some years there has been an increasing loss of respect for the Blessed Sacrament. The would-be worshipper can waste time searching round the church for the tabernacle. Congregations arrive and genuflect to the altar but the blessed Sacrament is not there. The move to diminish the significance of the Eucharist does not reflect the mood of the people, as is often claimed, but has been imposed on us by the authorities. I think they would say that it represents 'development of doctrine' but cannot be certain since they refuse to answer questions. Bishops in particular wax indignant when the laity shows signs of dissatisfaction with their dictates. Bishops appear to believe that they should command obedience no matter how whacky their notions. 'Theologians' of the modern cast do not care even for the word 'sacrament' and roll their eyes at the mention of transubstantiation. They would humanize religion to the extent where God is made in the image of man and does not exist outside the people. The emphasis at many 'masses' is no longer on the redemptive sacrifice of Calvary but on a 'shared meal', and there are priests who administer communion to anyone on the grounds, presumably, that it would be uncharitable to make distinctions.

However, the most remarkable bit of new-think on the Eucharist that I have read comes from an Anglican, the Rector of St James, Piccadilly. It seems that he has ventured into trade. It is a year since St James parochial church council set up a trading company to house a number of commercial activities. He has also become part owner of a coffee-house and has 'experienced some mild, friendly curiosity as to why a priest should be running a business: surely his work is with spiritual things?' Well, you would have thought so. You would have thought that all the cardinal works of mercy on top of organising services would have taken up most of a parson's time. But never mind that. Consider rather the Reverend's ideas on commerce and the body and blood of Christ. He writes in a parish chronicle, presumably with the intention of disarming criticism, that unease about his enterprises 'draws on one of the oldest heresies in Christianity: namely that God has no connection with material things, only with spirit ...' He goes on to announce that the Eucharist has come to mean more to him since his immersion in business. 'The denial of matter is clearly contradicted. The bread and wine are not just expressions of the bounty of God, they reflect different ways of productions (*sic*), distribution and exchange. The bread stands also for our exploitation of nature, the bitterness of competition, for business that makes the rich richer and the poor poorer. And wine is not just a symbol of freedom and joy, but of some of the most tragic forms of degradation, such as alcoholism, debt, broken relationships.' I have not the faintest idea what he means, although a worrying image of Christ in the Temple having a few words with the moneylenders keeps coming to mind. He continues: 'In the Eucharist it is all these material things that Jesus takes, saying "This is my body"; "This is my blood". The bread is broken in Christ's hands, our lives poured out in sacrifice with his, so they can become carriers of the power of God. In the taking, and the blessing, the breaking and sharing, a new creation is offered; there is a foretaste of all matter redeemed to its true and proper relation.

'In sharing in these mighty abstractions we can see powerful pointers to the possibility of business transformations towards the common good.'

I can't see it myself. And what's it got to do with cappuccino and cake?

5. CATHOLIC BISHOPS

While I could never imagine myself as a member of the C of E, I found the serialization of the life of Archbishop Runcie most interesting. He is an engaging character and his frankness – which I think he now perceives as indiscretion – is refreshing. After the wall of silence we meet from many Catholic bishops when we ask what is going on, it is pleasant to come across a cleric with a bit of mouth. Catholic bishops at the moment remind me of those shy wild creatures you occasionally catch a glimpse of – wide-eyed in the headlights before they scurry back to the hedgerow and the security of their own kind. They detest scrutiny, evade questioning and refuse to explain the twists and perversions of doctrine they seek to impose.

Listening one night, in my sleep, to the World Service I was awakened to full consciousness by a comment on European Catholicism. It was, said the speaker matter-of-factly, in a state of terminal decay and if Catholicism was to survive then it was up to people in other parts of the world to ensure that it should do so. We need a great wave of missionaries, particularly from Africa, to flood over and save our souls. One evening I went out for a drink with a Jewish friend. On our way home we passed my local church which, to my surprise, was lit up and resounding to music. At first I was suspicious, for certain clergy have been known to do strange things in this church: nothing like the Black Mass of course, but the building was long ago stripped of everything that made it specifically Catholic and on high and Holy days the kiddies make pictures of eggs or reindeer etc., and these are pinned to the walls, pillars and round the sanctuary to brighten the place up. One priest held remarkably loose views on the tenets of Christianity in general, and on at least one occasion celebrated Easter by getting everyone to dress up and scamper back and forth between the church and the community centre. There may have been more to it than that but whatever it was it was not obvious. And they have Lady Ministers of the Eucharist and guitars and other horrors that I prefer not to dwell on. However, on that night I was in for a joyful surprise. The place was crammed with Africans who had come from all over London to hear a visiting priest. I could not understand what he was saying for he spoke in his own tongue but there was a table full of literature – booklets, pamphlets and posters – and it was all totally doctrinally correct with never a hint of heresy. There were prayers to Our Lady and the Archangel Michael, both of whom are somewhat out of favour in certain circles; and there was an atmosphere of reverence and enthusiasm seldom encountered in these lukewarm times – unless you go somewhere where they fancy the Holy Ghost manifests himself in mass hysteria. This was an example of humanity with a proper awareness of God, neither arid nor mad, but reassured and reassuring. There were no self-consciously correct concessions to feminism or protestantism or modernism or monism, just a celebration of faith.

I once got into boiling water for pointing out that certain bishops were disobedient to Rome and were introducing peculiar practices: inviting unlikely characters to lecture, loosening the rules and taking a stunningly liberal view of what constituted proper sex education for small children. The only bishop I have felt real sympathy with in recent years is Eamonn Casey. He misbehaved and then said he was sorry. Bishops with ideas of their own splutter with fury should anyone suggest that they might have got it wrong. Apologize? Never. Offended silence or the threat of the lawsuit are the reward of the dissatisfied parishioner who does not wish to see his religion diluted with false ecumenism, heresy and a deal of codswallop. The C of E has long been skidding out of sight but nevertheless Archbishop Runcie should take heart. He has, at least, been frank and as such he comes across as delightfully original.

6. OPINIONS

❧ ✿ ❧

I get lots of letters. In one of them a Reverend writes: 'You may be a fine novelist but I really do wonder why your theological opinions should be of the slightest interest to anybody, let alone worthy of inclusion in *The Guardian*. Since you are not a professional theologian they are your private opinions ...' I had written a few words on the liberal approach to God, or as the Reverend would put it 'God', for on the reverse side of the letter is an ad for a work by the Reverend himself entitled *On Doing Without 'God'*. It is headed by a recommendation from Bishop Spong of Newark, New Jersey which calls to mind the old query: 'What's wrong with my hat, the cook admires it?' (The utterances of Bishop Spong used frequently to delight readers of *Private Eye*.) Part of the ad reads: 'In a global village, the God of religion should not be modelled in the metaphysical terms of a more parochial age. New ways of doing this must be developed.' New ways of doing *what*? However, the gratifying part of it is that I had written, in the article to which the Reverend takes such exception, about the intolerance of the liberal stance, the baffled outrage of the liberal whose views are questioned, the refusal to consider any other point of view. It is sweetly ironic that the modernists, the reformers, the liberals, say things like 'we are church', meaning presumably, the people, the laity. They wish to democratize the faith and give everyone a say except, of course, for the orthodox. The only voices the *bien pensant* can tolerate are those that sing in agreement with the current vogue, and the most noted 'professional theologians' of our time seem to be either feminists or atheists or both. The simple believer cannot get a word in.

The Reverend (who Bishop Spong compares to Nietzsche) concludes his rebuke with: 'and since your opinions appear on the face of it to be in conflict with nearly everybody since Augustine they are the expression of the purest protestantism.' Well I don't know about that. There are quite a lot of people since Augustine who think much as I do, and quite a lot of them are still around, much as they annoy the progressives. And *protestantism*? I expect the Rev means it in the wider sense since he so clearly disapproves. You can't win.

Let us turn from God to art, or possibly 'art'. I have before me a catalogue of the work of a lady who makes holes in bibles for reasons of her own: 'It's very pleasurable to drill a perfect hole.' It 'was an attempt to reinvent the bible with physicality. In a fetishistic way I have made a precious object of something close to hand'. She adds: 'When I drilled the bible, my mother asked me: "why have you done this?"' I do think that is such a good question. If I'd been her mother I would have asked the same and maybe smacked her. Having finished with the bible she took up a stretched cow's udder and was 'immediately inspired'. She said: 'It was the most exciting thing I had come across since Meret Oppenheimer's *Fur Teacup*. Seeing that a cow could be used for something other than producing milk was a total revelation'. A critic comments: 'The sexual charge in the udder-based work reaches a disturbing crescendo in *Trunk* which brings together in the confined space of an old wooden chest, a pair of women's knickers with a cow's teat sewn into the gusset.' He goes on about female sexuality and the pill and abortion and women's control over their own bodies and naturally Freud gets a mention, until the artist speaks again: 'This is the first and probably last time that I will place a cow's teat genitally, but it had to be done'. And they say the cows are mad. After this she takes up with snakes. 'The snake is a neutral thing sexually in that it is very difficult to tell the male from the female.' Except, presumably, for a snake. 'More than anything else I am interested in common mortality, common love and common struggle and the snake provides the perfect metaphor for that commonality ... They are very much together, these serpents, but they are also looking after their hearts'.

I don't think God is dead but art is clearly far from well.

7. RUBBISHING RELIGION

I once interviewed the head of an airline. He had been a pilot but was now, as it were, elevated to a different kind of power. As the interview progressed it became clear that he was relieved to be sitting behind a desk rather than at the controls of an aeroplane. Flying, he said, was dangerous, adding that it was boring. He told me several things I would have preferred not to know, especially as I was due to fly home on one of his planes. He told me that the co-pilot was usually disgruntled because he wasn't the pilot and the pilot was usually looking eagerly forward to retirement. He said that anyone who wanted to fly a large, dangerous, boring aeroplane must be slightly mad and that there were, in fact, people up there who were very mad. He said something to the effect that the technology involved was now so complex that no one person could grasp it, and that if anything should go awry it was beyond the competence of humankind to correct it. He gave examples of the eccentricity of pilots he had known, and all in all, demolished what dubious faith I had in air travel. Not a reassuring man.

Something my eldest son told me this morning reminded me of this person. The son had sat up late watching a chat show whereon a cleric, clad in traditional fashion with purple shirt, socks etc., had enthusiastically rubbished 'religion', saying the word was unknown in the Bible. This urge to hack away at your own foundations is misguided and can only leave the populace anxious and unsure. The hackers, I imagine, believe themselves to be acting in an honest, open and democratic fashion.

The same sort of thing has been happening in certain schools where the concept of authority causes the liberal to totter back, aghast. Trouble ensues. In the last issue of *The Oldie* the excellent Dr Stuttaford described how the depressed person goes to bed early, goes to sleep immediately, then wakes up for the rest of the night. I do that. Then I twiddle the knobs on the wireless in search of something interesting if not uplifting. The other night I heard yet another chat-show host talking about the present school crisis and giving it as his opinion that all children were born good. I can understand why people have this superficial impression: babies, on the whole, appear harmless with their big eyes and their sweet little noses and their first adorable smiles. But I have known a lot of children and behind their enchanting exterior lies Original Sin. This cannot be caned out of them. They need guidance and example and education. They will not learn to read if they are not taught and many of them will see no reason to refrain from torturing the cat unless they are told not to. I happen to know this for a fact, having had experience on the shop floor. So please will new management not try to tell me any different.

Management in every sphere seems to be increasingly out of touch with reality and theories are no substitute for actuality. Anyway they are usually wrong and will have to be regularly reversed, which is a waste of effort, time and money and lowers general morale. I would rather follow a believing priest than have him tell me that God doesn't exist or is within me, or possibly both. We keep putting our faith in the wrong box and the skies are darkening, so as it's getting on for 6pm, I think I'll go to bed.

8. THE GREAT TERESA

I wish somebody would tell me why the banned video *Visions of Ecstasy* is thought to be about St Teresa of Avila. It features a babe sparsely hung about in remnants of some theatrical costumier's notion of what constitutes a nun's clothing, bearing no relation whatsoever to the Carmelite habit, and shows the silly girl sticking a nail in her hand. A minor detail, you might think, but St Teresa did not have the stigmata. St Teresa was a woman of consummate common sense, hard working, practical and witty. She was sceptical about mystical experience, frequently seeking reassurance that her opinions were not self or – more alarming – demonically induced and spent most of her life shaking up and reforming various convents where laxity and profligacy had taken hold. She wrote: 'When enraptured how conscious the soul becomes of being imprisoned in the body and of the wretchedness of this life. It is as though sold into slavery in a foreign land', and 'The best prayer, that most pleasing to God, is that which produces the best results in good works, not that which we enjoy with no other effect but our own satisfaction.' Hardly the message of *Visions of Ecstasy*, which is a soggy representation of lesbianism and sado-masochism.

St Teresa was wont to exclaim 'May God preserve us from stupid nuns', and it is intriguing to speculate on what she would have said of this video. Her first requirement when admitting novices to the new foundations was *intelligence* – a quality markedly absent from *Visions of Ecstasy* – for, 'Even though our Lord should give this young girl devotion and teach her contemplation, if she has no sense she never will come to have any, and instead of being of use to the community she will be a burden!' No, I cannot imagine her reaction to the carryings-on in the video.

There has been much talk about blasphemy and the right to free expression, but what is really irritating about the film is its idiocy. No one seems to mind about that or the perpetuation of ignorance and uninformed prejudice. I do not believe that Nigel

Wingrove, the director, had ever heard of Teresa of Avila until some ass mentioned her. He says, rather sweetly, that his work is obscure and he himself 'a silly nobody'. Blasphemy is rife, but although foul, it is not as dangerous as the insidious, encroaching heresy now afflicting the Church, all attributable to a lack of education and a failure of common sense. Nor with all the talk of freedom of expression has anyone thought to make the point that slander, as distinct from blasphemy, is offensive not only to the victim, alive or dead, but to the victim's friends. We are entitled to take umbrage when someone we respect is portrayed as a half-witted slapper. It is incumbent on us to protest. It is natural and wholesome to manifest resentment when you see the reputation of those you love being distorted by lies and perverse fantasy. *Visions of Ecstasy* is too slight, too mindless and foolish to be taken seriously as blasphemy, but it is infuriating that it should be thought of as having any connection with the great Teresa.

Let her have the last word. A lawyer was once rude to her (intrepid fellow), and she said: 'Sir, may God return to you the courtesy you have shown to me.'

9. PECULIAR

Christianity is in a peculiar state, especially here in the USA, although having said that I must admit it's in a pretty odd state back home, what with the new C of E logo and the Bad Hair Day ad, and the Sea of Faith and the various atheistic clergymen one encounters from time to time. An accountant who found himself suddenly innumerate or a butcher who felt inclined to vegetarianism would surely resign and seek employment in another field. It would only be fair to the poor bewildered customers.

I came across another twist in tradition over Christmas as I watched American TV. Several programmes about the life of Jesus told us confidently that he was the eldest of a large family with four brothers and two sisters called Lydia and Anna, which makes him into someone with whom I am entirely unfamiliar. The idea, I think, is to make Mary more 'relevant' to modern women but I couldn't swear to it. It certainly knocks the petals off centuries of faith. The biblical scholars are to blame. They have to give themselves something to do and when in doubt invent a new yarn out of whole cloth, as it were. The new versions are nothing like as compelling as the original and the sheep, finding themselves in arid pasture bereft of all spiritual nourishment, amble sheepily off to what appear to be greener fields.

There are many of these in Los Angeles; churches of every conceivable flavour offering everything the modern human heart could desire, from wealth and fame to a cure for cancer and bunions and foolproof recipes for perfect human relationships. You might be tempted if you hadn't seen it all before, sometimes failing spectacularly with mass suicides and sometimes withering quietly away. The tried and proved is no longer enough as novelty is perceived as progress and the hungry fall for false promises. Many of the new movements make concessions to feminist aspirations, though not always whole-heartedly. Some of the radio preachers clearly have old fashioned ideas about 'women's place' while trying not to say so.

With all the talk of equality there is an uneasy, pervasive air of hostility and misunderstanding between the sexes. The more it is repressed the more it becomes evident. Women having invented the fantastical concept of New Man are cross when he fails to live up to expectations and men are not at all sure what they're supposed to do, often taking refuge in aggrieved silence. The re-writing of history and the attempt to re-structure human nature could drive us all mad.

Even the weather shows signs of unrest with rain and gales in LA, sun and snow in Texas. This may gratify those of a chiliastic disposition who are standing round on mountains, shifting from foot to foot expecting the end of the world, but it makes it hard to know what to put on in the morning. One does sometimes yearn for the old certainties.

10. OH GOD

Oh God – and I mean that. Oh *God*. I went to Mass in Texas, to
a church built in the new Catholic mode: spectacularly drab,
boring, barren and constructed 'in the round', probably at vast
expense, while the original church was either demolished or
left to fall over. The idea is that the priest should not appear
exclusive or in any way elevated above the flock, which ideally
should sit round him in a circle like a pack of hyenas. However,
since he is not made Janus-like with a face on the back of his
head, in order to be fully inclusive he would need to spin like a
ballerina throughout the course of the service. In view of some
of the antics congregations have been subjected to I would not
be inordinately astonished if this came to pass, but at present
the little problem is resolved by arranging the faithful in a sort
of uneasy banana-shape. We were greeted at the door with a
handshake from a lay person, in this case a man, and when we
were seated we were welcomed by a lady standing in front of
one end of the banana while the priest was situated at the other
end. Behind the lady sat the choir. At this point I went into my
customary trance, which is the only way I can endure the 'New
Mass' without exclaiming aloud at the liturgical dog's breakfast
the 'reformers' have made out of the rite. I was roused at the
onset of the Gloria when the congregation began a rhythmic
clapping and again at the Our Father when they all held hands.
Then came the 'sign of peace' where everyone has to shuffle,
stretch and twist (grinning the while) in order to press as much
flesh as is humanly possible. Everyone took communion (in the
hand, naturally) except for me, because far from being in a state
of grace I was in a state of embarrassed fury. I feel much the
same when I go to children's parties and have to wear a funny
hat and join in 'Old McDonald Had a Farm'. I'm not five years
old, for God's sake. 'Ugh', I said as I sidled out past the priest,
who was now the one trying to shake everyone's hand. 'Didn't
you like that?' asked our friend, surprised. 'No', I said. He
enquired wheth_____ t preferable to sitting in silence at

the back of a cathedral. 'No,' I said again. I have given up trying to explain to the younger generation that we are not mere passive spectators at the Tridentine Mass but deeply involved in the mystery, the holiness, the sense of awe, the awareness of a Presence which you sure as hell don't feel in the kindergarten atmosphere that too often prevails now. With all the endless talk of 'empowering the laity', of giving us a 'role in church affairs', we have ended up being treated like witless kiddies, too stupid, too immature to grasp anything smacking of theological complexity: everything must be sweetened, diluted, simplified and made as bland as infants' pap. No guilt and certainly no humility and nothing that might appear to tax our intelligence. The attitude of the 'reformers' is profoundly insulting, *patronising* in the worst possible way, and if we complain they take offence, protesting crossly that it's all for our own good and how can we be so ungrateful?' The changes in the Church increasingly look less like alteration than total destruction, an act of iconoclasm, vandalism previously unsurpassed.

Afterwards we went out to lunch and had chicken-fried steak in a bun with chips. It was extremely disgusting which seemed somehow not unfitting. A sadly nauseous day all round – or maybe banana shaped. Oh *God*.

11. THE PURE SPIRIT

The other day I was attempting to tidy up some papers. It has to be done, at least once in a lifetime, but I'd rather tackle the municipal dump. And now the urge to offer a piece of advice has come upon me: if you are bereaved and have a house full of letters and photographs, get someone else to do it. Doing it myself, I was reminded of these stories of people stranded alone in the wilderness who, meeting with some mishap, operate on themselves with a rusty penknife. If you must you must, but better not. The older letters are less painful and can prove diverting. Among a pile of bills, bus tickets, etc., I found some letters written to my parents when I was born. They were all from members of the Church of Humanity, an earnest and high-minded group which my father had joined in his youth. One of these epistles expressed regret that the writer, a woman, had been unavoidably prevented from decorating the altar in preparation for my reception into the Church, and I was puzzled. I vaguely knew that the building had been adorned with busts of worthy human beings – Plato and such like, and the founder Auguste Comte – but I had not known there was an altar. Altars have only one purpose after all: the making of offerings to God or whatever gods you happen to favour, so what was it doing in this temple of humanity? What did they sacrifice on this altar? Who did they worship and why did they follow so closely the rituals of religion? Were they atheists or did they believe that man was God? I find the works of Comte impenetrable and his obsession with his lady friend Clothilde hopelessly comic, so there is no enlightenment from the source. Does anyone know what was going on? Another letter addressed to the infant that I was ends with the words: 'May all the blessings of humanity fall upon you!' Thanks very much, I thought, up to my knees in reminders of loss, mingling with ancient tax demands and acres of bureaucratic jiggery-pokery, and wishing I was formed of pure spirit. I am baffled by humanity's admiration of itself and its works. Does it not listen to the news or take a good look round now and then? What reason does it have to be so pleased with itself? I heard a man on the wireless recently talking about his idea of Utopia, and listening between the lines, it was possible to discern the underlying unacknowledged dream of all Utopians – not that he might live in peace with his neighbour, but that the neighbour, who has conflicting ideas of his own, might conveniently cease to be, leaving the Utopian with the place to himself. It is a baby's dream and quite impracticable, not the mature vision that the humanist would have us strive after. Utopia, on the whole, sounds far more boring and lowering to the spirits than the most harp-infested image of heaven. Man with some concept of god-given law is bad enough, but the thought of man alone making up the rules as he goes along is too frightening to contemplate. As Edith Wharton observed: 'Man's relation to his self-imposed laws shows how little human conduct is generally troubled by its own sanctions.'

One of the things I was looking for in all these papers was my husband's translation of Erasmus's *Praise of Folly* but he must have destroyed the manuscript before he died. He never finished it to his own satisfaction, but I think the decision to bin it was a mistaken form of pride. Wildly annoying.

12. FALSE MESSIAHS

I have just received a letter from a friend in America. He is affronted by the reaction of the English press to the fate of the people of Heaven's Gate, finding the mirthful tone unseemly. Alas, ever since the Reformation numberless cults and false messiahs have made their appearance in this country and the overall response has always been one of hilarity, often mixed, I fear, with punitive contempt. In a book, *English Messiahs*, by Ronald Matthews, published in 1936, the author begins, 'The pretension to be Christ, His Mother, or a special messenger from Him is naturally quite a popular one in a Christian, and more particularly, a Protestant country.' This, he argues, is a consequence of the Protestant belief in religious individualism.

In the time of the Commonwealth, many people, deprived of the feasts of the Church and the former sports and games of the country, turned with lively enthusiasm to their own interpretations of the newly translated scriptures. There arose, to mention but a few, Muggletonians who held that their prophet heralded a fresh phase of the Christian era, Fifth Monarchy men who looked for the speedy establishment of the millennium, Ranters who claimed that Cain was the third member of the Trinity and Quakers of varying views fighting among themselves. One of them, James Nayler, 1618–1660, had the misfortune to attract to himself 'a group of unbalanced female admirers of a type that still plagues the life of well-looking ministers of religion.' These ladies, with their faith in the doctrine of Inner Light, persuaded Nayler, against his better judgement, that he was Jesus, explaining their extravagance of feeling as the promptings of the Spirit. They escorted him into Bristol on a horse with cries of Holy, Holy and Hosannah. The populace laughed but poor Nayler was convicted of blasphemy; he was whipped, and had his tongue bored through with a hot iron.

Then there was Joanna Southcott, the Bride of the Lamb, who in 1814 announced that God had told her, 'This year, in the 65th year of my age, thou shalt have a Son by the power of the Most

High, which if the Jews receive as their Prophet, Priest and King, then I will restore them to their own land and cast out the heathen for their sakes.' A splendid crib was prepared at a cost of £200 and put on display, but Joanna died childless leaving her followers in disarray. The famous Great Box of Sealed Writings containing prophecies had disappeared. Everybody laughed. Richard Brothers, 1757–1824, declared himself, 'God Almighty's Nephew', which at least has the virtue of originality. He proceeded to get himself into trouble by writing, 'The Lord God commands me to say to you, George III, King of England, that immediately on my being revealed in London to the Hebrews as their Prince and to all nations as their Governor, your power must be delivered up to me ...' The King, in a rare moment of lucidity, demanded that something be done about Brothers. He was tried for treason but found, not unreasonably, to be insane.

Even madder and far more dangerous was one John Nichols Tom, the son of a publican. He adopted the title of Sir William Percy Honeywood Courtenay, Knight of Malta, Earl of Devon, King of Jerusalem and of the Gypsies; finally claiming, 'Christ dwells in my body, I am the temple of the Holy Ghost.' Telling his peasant followers that he and they were invulnerble, he led them into battle with the red-coats and eight of them were killed. So was their messiah. There were countless other leaders, all seeming to have the ability to attract money and women – which led to frightful misunderstandings and entanglements. In 1902, the Reverend John Hugh Smyth Piggot declared himself the Lord Jesus Christ, 'Yes, I am he that liveth, and behold I am alive for evermore.' He caused a commotion by proposing to turn the pond on Clapton Common into wine and then walk on it. Thousands turned up to jeer and Smyth Piggot had to be escorted home in a carriage surrounded by mounted police. He had taken a 'spiritual bride' who went on to have three children named Glory, Power and Life. He was eventually unfrocked for immorality, a gentler conclusion than torture or mass suicide; but clearly, new religion should come labelled with a health warning.

13. PAGANS

Going through the bookshelves the other day, I found an interesting work entitled *The Graces of Interior Prayer*. Good, I said to myself, I will share the insights of this book with the readers of *The Oldie*. (I didn't actually say that out loud, it was merely an intention and I never use the word 'share' unless I'm giving Smarties to children, but I meant well.) Picture my annoyance when, on returning to the shelf in question, I could not find the book. It is not the sort of book which is in great demand, so I can only assume that I have put it somewhere safe and it will either turn up again one day in the sock drawer, or it won't.

In the meantime, I shall address myself briefly to the topic of paganism. Flicking through the TV channels one dull afternoon, I came across a woman bewailing the fate of an Inca King. His only fault, she announced pitifully, was that he had been a pagan and the mean invaders had gone and killed him. Now it was only a short while since I had seen another programme in which was described the fate of an Inca child; he had been sacrificed to the Inca gods and had died in dreadful terror, covered in vomit and diarrhoea, so the notion of those sweet, old, peaceful pagans needs some adjustment.

W. Arens in 1979 held that tales of cannibalism among, for instance, the Aztecs, were a libellous fabrication invented by the Spanish to justify their own, admittedly often regrettable, behaviour. Eye-witness evidence of the 16th century was discounted as spiteful gossip. This view provoked further research and it became clear that our ancestors, right back to the Stone Age, did eat each other, not only on the possibly reasonable grounds that they needed the protein, but for ritual purposes. In 1521, 62 Spanish soldiers were sacrificed to the Aztec gods; their hearts were ripped out and offered to the sun, Xippili, Quauhtlevaintl. The hearts were called 'precious eagle-cactus fruit' and 'they offered it to him; they nourished him ...' The author of this account estimated one pile of human skulls as numbering more than 100,000. The limbs of the captives, and other bits, were cooked with peppers and tomatoes and served as topping on plates of maize. Montezuma himself was offered a thigh from each corpse, while the rest was 'shared' out among the elite.

According to the *Encyclopaedia Britannica*, 'It was not merely for conquest and tribute that the fierce Mexicans ravaged their neighbour-lands, but they had a stronger motive than either in the desire to obtain multitudes of prisoners whose hearts were to be torn out by the sacrificing priests to propitiate a pantheon of gods who well personified their bloodthirsty worshippers. The desire for war-captives as acceptable victims is related to have brought about an almost incredible agreement among the nations of the Mexican alliance, that they should, from time to time, fight battles among themselves in order to provide prisoners for the altars.' The behaviour of our own football hooligans and certain other groups might lead us to suppose that the instinct for battle, albeit on different grounds, is not as far below the surface as we like to imagine. Simultaneously, we have around new pagans who claim that formal religion is repressive and bad for us, and that the revival or, as some would have it, the continuation of practices like witchcraft is a force only for good. Moses, to mention but one who was at pains to disabuse the people of the value of paganism, must be tearing his beard out.

14. DRESS AS YOU PLEASE

A nun was talking recently about the scarcity of vocations. The person to whom she spoke asked her what she was doing to encourage new recruits. The nun said enthusiastically that they'd already rid themselves of the time-hallowed habit, and were thinking up various wheezes to coax young women into their reduced community. She chose to ignore the fact that, previous to the changes, there was no noticeable shortage of vocations. The 'reformers' like to pretend that there was, and that had there been no upheaval, the Church would have withered away – which is the opposite of the truth. Looking at the facts dispassionately, one can conclude that the reformers were intent on destroying the Church and putting something else in its place. Contemplating the 'new' nun, one can only wonder what self-respecting female in her right mind would dream of joining her.

Much of the appeal of the religious life used to lie in the challenge it presented. It took courage and determination, as well as faith, to abandon what the world perceived as desirable, and the distinctive habit was an outward sign of commitment. Besides, if one may be permitted to strike a fashion note, the habit suited all women regardless of size, shape or form of countenance, and was a pleasure to gaze upon. A group of nuns clad in the old style, compared with the new ones in short skirts, anoraks, lisle stockings, sandals and the unbecoming approximation of a veil, are reminiscent of swans adjacent to a bunch of tatty pigeons. Some new nuns, of course, dress as they please, with make-up, hair-dos and earrings, and God alone knows what message they hope to put across. I think they might claim that the inner light of the spirit shines through their outer appearance, but it doesn't. Many of them are concerned only with feminism, goddesses and 'women's rites' – which is even more tiresome than the eldritch squawking about 'rights', and flesh-creepingly silly. Not just spirituality, but all common sense disappears in a welter of secular trendiness, hung about with the tawdry baubles of paganism which are intended, I suppose, to add a flavour of other-worldliness, but are in direct contradiction to Christianity. One of the troubles with the devil is that he has lousy taste; he is not the suave gentleman that some would like to think of him as, but a poseur avid to keep up to date with the latest fad. I sometimes think that perhaps he lives in Islington and reads *The Tablet*, but I may be doing him an injustice.

But back to the subject of dress. Picture if you will an exquisite robe, crafted with infinite care, designed to fit perfectly the form for which it was intended, glorious in colour and texture, jewelled, embroidered and implicit with significance. Comfortable too. Then imagine a new designer armed with a pair of state-of-the-art shears. 'Don't worry,' says this person, 'I'm not going to alter its basic integrity, I'm just going to tidy it up a little, make it more relevant.' Snip, go the shears, off with the hem, replaced with a strip of day-glo nylon. Then he (or she – I haven't discerned the sex of this person) decides that embroidery is old-fashioned, so it gets ripped out. Then the jewels. Jewels give an impression of elitism; they have to go. In the attempt to disguise his ravages our designer tears out the front and replaces it with yards of crimplene, then hacks off the back and the sleeves and tacks in some bubble-wrap and oven-foil. In case it looks dull, he sticks Christmas tree decorations all over it and announces a new beginning.

Some people accept this travesty and clap their hands and swoon in spurious ecstasy. The majority, who don't, are told off for 'clinging to the past'. How much happier we should have been if the designer had merely fashioned for himself another garment out of the old newspapers and cardboard boxes more suited to his intentions. Tradition is allied to eternity, while the curse of our age – fashion– must fade, and a good thing too. The animation claimed for the new robe is probably caused by the stirring of hot and sulphurous winds. (As I wrote those rude words about Satan, the adversary, my pen dried up. Typical petty spite.)

15. INFORMALITY

A child visiting his (Catholic) prep school for the first time was favourably impressed by many of its aspects but the thing that most surprised him was the action of his schoolboy neighbour at lunch. The boy, without prompting, poured him a glass of water. The aforesaid child, who has been largely brought up in the US of A, is not unusually ill-mannered, and nor are his friends, but they are unaccustomed to such simple acts of courtesy, having been trained in the belief that if you want anything in this world you'd better go out and get it for yourself. Otherwise your independence and self-esteem might suffer, and you might end up at the bottom of the pile. This view co-exists uneasily with the idea that we all really love and are well-disposed to each other, and is further confused by the spirit of competition which prevails in America. The child later proceeded to surprise the rest of us by taking not only his own used plate out to the scullery, but also that of his small cousin. A trivial matter, you might think, but a step in the right direction. The motto 'God helps those who help themselves' is unedifying and hardly Christian. I improved the shining hour by going on about the monastic tradition of courtesy in which you were encouraged, if not compelled, to put others first and to be alert to all their needs, while never imposing yourself on their attention.

Since the 1960s, a less formal code has been in vogue. In place of politeness we are all expected to manifest affection for each other, no matter how spurious. We awkwardly exchange the 'sign of peace', twisting and shuffling and baring our teeth, prey to the notion that we all need physical contact and that touching is healthy. Naturally, this has led to numerous misunderstandings and much embarrassment. The Methodists have belatedly realized that promiscuous cuddling, even in a religious context, can be misconstrued as sexual harassment and have decided to limit it, but we are all sadly mixed up. Extreme, formal politeness can be chilling – a sign of exclusivity and a form of cruelty – but most of us have no desire to be hugged by strangers even while we are being assured that we are all the people of God. We may be, but the relationship is best expressed in spiritual rather than physical terms. Before so many daft ideas sprang up in the aftermath of Vatican II, physical contact was forbidden in religious communities, not out of an inhuman puritanism, but because centuries of experience had shown that it was in the interests of peace and harmony. As the moderns would put it – everyone needs his own space. Or perhaps *her* own space, which brings us to women and the way so many have ceased to mind their manners.

'The perfect woman nobly planned' is out of fashion and the scantily clad wench with her lower jaw jutting threateningly is the role model for what the Victorians called 'our girls'. No self-respecting female aspires to be a gentlewoman. Certain nuns and feminist theologians are among the most aggressive, leaving even the Spice Girls in the shade. They don't, on the whole, go round hitting people or carrying knives, but they are very rude about anyone who fails to see their point, especially men about whom they grumble endlessly. St Augustine has drawn censure upon himself for his observations on birth and the female anatomy, but he spoke no more than the truth. Ask any midwife. Our girls have lost touch with both religion and reality, and few of them would have much in common with the woman at the well. They would be more likely, one suspects, to push the man to one side with the demand: 'Make mine a double.'

16. CONTRADICTORY MESSAGES

Sending out contradictory messages is an effective way of driving people mad. 'Now don't touch those,' says the cook as she puts a plate of fragrant smelling cakes fresh from the oven on the table. You can't open a magazine or watch TV without being exhorted to buy something silly which you can't afford and isn't good for either you or society. A new car (we must reduce the traffic on roads). Alcohol (drink is deleterious to the system and leads to increased crime). Sweets (sugar rots the teeth). Meat (be careful, BSE, E coli, cholesterol). Jeans (you'd better give up the sweets if you want to fit into them). Everything is guaranteed to poison you slightly, destroy the environment or cause dissatisfaction to the under-privileged or the overweight, while being presented as not only desirable but essential. The populace reads about the ill-gotten gains and goings-on of the rich and when it tries a bit of benefit fraud or theft of its own, is both bewildered and aggrieved when called to account. It's not fair, the people protest and you can just discern their point. Even the level of violence is more understandable when you can spend every night watching actors bashing seven bells out of each other without much altering the set of their features. There are still those who insist that we are unaffected by what we see and read, but if that were so, the advertising agencies would long since have folded up their tents and stolen away. We are reduced to stating the obvious and sitting back in quiet despair.

Our leaders tell us that the country is doing well and there is scope for optimism, but I don't think the unemployed and the homeless are convinced. It's not much use telling people to get a job when all the jobs are being done by computers. Our leaders are too fond of denying that anything is amiss. The Churches also blandly deny that they are in disarray, in the teeth of the evidence. Certain forces in the Catholic Church, have been endeavouring to promulgate what I think they consider is an enlightened attitude to sexuality, and have gone over the edge (a common danger in liberalism). There have been some hair-raisingly explicit sex education programmes in the USA and inevitably their influence has crept over here. Small children are fed information they do not yet need and can't do much with. Most parents, certainly the ones I know, are not in favour of this move.

There is great revulsion towards paedophilia in this country, yet children are covertly encouraged to experiment, which can only be good news for the paedophile who is usually convinced that his actions are harmless anyway. Some years ago Dr Jack Dominian reviewed a book called *Childhood and Sexuality: A Radical Christian Approach*. He wrote of the author, 'he is compassionate to paedophilic tendencies in which he takes particular pain to distinguish what he considers the love of children by men who are gentle and shy, and the viciousness of those who seduce children for sadistic reasons.' One can picture the paedophile weighing up his own inclinations and in all probability putting himself in the first category. So that's all right then. More recently Peter Tatchell wrote, 'it is time society acknowledged the truth that not all sex involving children is unwanted, abusive and harmful.' But on the evidence it most certainly is.

Another muddle: a woman of 33 who goes away with a 14-year-old boy is vilified, while a 'Love Bus' tours the coast handing out condoms to under-age children. In the States, paedophile Christian priests, who had doubtless taken notice of the above liberal opinions, land the Church with a multi-million dollar bill for compensation. As a friend remarked thoughtfully on hearing the amounts involved, 'The rent boys must be grinding their teeth in rage.' Contradictory messages will have us all gibbering by the end of the century.

17. FINISHING THE JOB

When the Red Guard of the Church, in the wake of Vatican II, had more or less completed the work of destruction begun in the Reformation, tidying up any little corners where iconoclasm might not have found full expression, I wondered whether they might now ask themselves a few questions. After all, their stated aim had been to 'let air' into the Church, encouraging, presumably, new adherents who might previously have been frightened off. Since the result of their endeavours has been an unprecedented drop in Mass attendance, a near terminal decline in vocations, the closure of religious foundations and schools, and widespread despair among the faithful, one might have expected some soul-searching, or, since the concept of soul is also in doubt in certain circles, at least a little perplexed head-scratching. Surely this could not have been what they intended?

But who knows? Theologians, bishops, elderly nuns, busybody laymen, the army of religious termites seem smugly content with the damage they have wrought. We shouldn't be surprised. We have the constant example before us of inept or corrupt politicians who make our lives a misery with their meddling and always appear self-satisfied, or else deeply aggrieved at being called to account. The reformer is incapable of introspection. Pol Pot on TV represented himself as a much misunderstood man whose fine intentions had been wilfully misconstrued; while another, when it was put to him that millions of his countrymen had been murdered, laughed merrily. No, not millions – thousands maybe. An extreme example but typical.

Here, it is the modernizers and the liberals from whom we have the most to fear. The liberal stands in the midst of ruin, patting himself on the back and insisting that all is well. Guilt belongs to the past. While the technically blameless fly around apologising for matters over which they had no control, since the events occurred in a different time and climate and were perpetrated by others, no one in the present will accept responsibility for anything.

They meant well, they say: they know they were right and so their theories and actions can have had only a beneficial effect. Forget the evidence. New is good and old is bad. To some minds it seems that good is bad and bad is good. Holiness is in disrepute. Sanctity is personal and therefore, by definition, elitist and exclusive. We are all only human and for anyone to aim high in anything but worldly terms is demeaning to the rest. It makes them uncomfortable. Sob and hug in groups and go about in vari-coloured ribbons but go no further alone or you will be outcast, as many unwary Christians have found. Simply admit to being only human and you can do more or less as you like without censure, but do not aspire to be more than usually good. This is regarded as unhealthy. Poverty, chastity and obedience, for example, are particularly abhorrent, both to the leaders of fashion, secular and religious, and to the herd.

Beauty is out of style and distortion is in vogue. Once the churches might have been expected to withstand the trend but now they are entranced by innovation. The C of E is still busily hacking away at its own foundations although it has already more or less demolished itself and the heretical element in the RC Church is not far behind. Instead of doing what they are supposed to do, which is to lead and inspire, the church authorities scuttle to the rear of the crowd, adopt the latest poodle cut and cravenly follow the trend. You'd think the least we could expect would be an 'oops, sorry', but we'll never hear it. Not until the present is in the past and only then if the devil hasn't got us all. I would apologize for this Jeremiah-like stance but the personal *mea culpa* is so un-chic at present that I cannot bring myself to do so.

18. SOUR

I spent the weeks before Christmas looking sideways at hoardings and skimming nervously through newspapers in case the churches came up with some brilliant new wheeze to interest us all in the meaning of Christmas and the deeper significance of the Christian religion. Last year we had 'Bad Hair Day?', a campaign which tried to seize the attention of the uncommitted by suggesting wittily that little could be worse than being a virgin, finding you were pregnant and, what's more, there were three kings coming to dinner. The year before there were posters littered about stating that Christians made better lovers, a jest in dubious taste; and one year some lady proposed earnestly that mention of the Crucifixion should be omitted from Easter because the spectacle of a tortured man was too depressing at a time of festivity.

This time the producers of nativity plays were instructed to leave out the three kings because they weren't there and anyway, they weren't kings. We've always known that they got there late, adding their representation to the group round the crib at Epiphany, but you can't expect the audience at a nativity play to hang about for days waiting for the rest of the cast to arrive. Poetic licence must sometimes be allowed precedence over literal interpretation. The German approach to hermeneutics leaves a lot to be desired. The problem could be overcome by having a kiddy step forward to introduce the Magi with the words, 'Some time later ...', a simple device, if old-fashioned, which did much to elucidate matters in early black and white films.

There are plenty of other sources of irritation and mystification in current religious affairs. One of the new career nuns writes that she once saw an unsmiling photograph of Mother Teresa in which she looked positively 'sour'. I don't know where the idea arose that saints should go about with a permanent beatific smirk pasted on their faces, but it is very unrealistic. Most people look sour at some time, especially if they're extremely aged, have worked every hour that God sent, have more things to do and there's a photographer pointing a camera at their nose. The niggling urge to denigrate Mother Teresa seems ineradicable in some quarters.

The feminists also have little time for Our Lady and keep banging on about the feminine nature of God. They seem to see God's mother as a sort of secretary, bustling about making the tea and filing things, while they wish to identify with the person in the boss's chair. To this end, some of them refer to Him – or rather her, since they have abandoned all pretence – as 'Our Sweet Sophia', taking a characteristic of the Divinity as a whole and making it female in actual rather than grammatical terms. Others, men as well as women, attempting to be more circumspect, seem to imply that God is half and half, and just as much female as male. The problem with this doubtless well-intentioned idea is that the human mind is not, on the whole, constructed to assimilate it. Presented with this androgynous image, in place of the paternal, the incorrigible human mind tends to conjure up a figure on the lines of Lily Savage which is not edifying.

It is simpler to admit that we cannot begin to comprehend the nature of God, whose thoughts are not our thoughts, nor His ways our ways, and to accept the advice of Christ that we should say 'Our Father...' He had no trouble distinguishing between His parents and He should know.

19. I'LL BLOW THE
DAMN THING UP

ᥴ᥈ᥣ᥋

Mother Angelica is an American nun in the orthodox Catholic tradition. She is also the founder and chief executive officer of the Eternal Word Television network, 'a TV station which reaches 40 million homes from coast to coast right across America, and 13.5 million homes in 30 other countries.' A Poor Clare, she wears the unreconstructed habit and is living proof that nuns don't have to look like something the cat dragged out of the reject shop in order to get things done in the modern world. And she doesn't mince her words. She is quite clear about the Faith and she says what she means, which is not as usual in current church affairs as you might suppose were you not paying attention.

Last November she annoyed Cardinal Mahoney of the largest Catholic diocese in the US by criticizing his attitude to the Eucharist. She said that his teaching that the bread and wine remained 'unchanged' after consecration was confusing for Catholics. If she lived in that diocese, she said, her obedience would be absolutely zero and she hoped the people of the diocese felt the same way. With magnificent predictability the Cardinal rose to the bait and demanded a public apology, describing her attack as 'astounding and reprehensible'. 'Your call for my people to offer zero obedience to their shepherd is unheard of and shocking.'

A poll conducted for the *New York Times* in April 1994 found that only 34 per cent of Catholics believed that the bread and wine becomes the body and blood of Christ at the Eucharist, while 63 per cent said that they are merely symbolic reminders of Jesus. It seems the Cardinal intends to go sobbing to Rome with his wounded feelings, but who, one asks oneself, is responsible for the above curious state of affairs?

The Church leaders, that's who. In their passion for modernism, ecumenism and various other dubious *isms*, they have

37

watered down doctrine to homeopathic proportions while simultaneously insisting that they haven't. The Cardinal's howls of protest have quite rightly failed to impress or intimidate Mother Angelica. Too many cardinals, bishops and priests demand obedience to themselves and their views rather than to the tenets of the Faith, but according to Canon 212, the Code of Canon Law, Christ's faithful 'have the right, indeed at times the duty, in keeping with their knowledge, competence and position, to manifest to the sacred Pastors their views on matters which concern the good of the Church', which advice, when implemented, frequently makes the aforesaid Pastors hopping mad, but who cares. Too many of them have betrayed us.

Mother Angelica, in an earlier difference of opinion with members of the hierarchy, refused to interview three or four of them at the bishops' conference. They got 'very angry' and asked, 'By what authority do you do that?' She responded that she owned the network. 'Well', said one, with what sounded like sour satisfaction, 'you won't always be there'. To which the sublime Angelica retorted, 'Well, I'll blow the damn thing up before you get it'. In an arid and useless atmosphere of appeasement (commonly referred to as ecumenism) and blatant doublespeak, such forthrightness is refreshing.

20. JEREMIAH

⏤⏤✿⏤⏤

Prophets of doom have seldom been popular. They have had their adherents, usually people who saw no good reason why the world and time should continue: their businesses or crops had failed, their relationships were unsatisfactory, other people were having all the fun and there seemed no good reason why everything should not be consumed by flood or fire with the four horsemen adding to the confusion, accompanied by much wailing and gnashing of teeth.

There was also the simple pessimist who, while not desiring calamity, saw something nasty as inevitable and incipient. Then there were a few rational beings who looked at the evidence and the way matters were progressing and pronounced the prognosis poor. There seem to be more of these around today but they lack the glamour of the inspired prophet, whiskers whirling in the wind, voice booming down the avenues of graven images and through the habitations of the harlot or whatever. This type of prophet usually had a rough passage in biblical times, whereas his present day counterpart in the Bible belt seems to enjoy a privileged lifestyle. It is all most baffling. The scientist who warns us that our consumption of energy will lead to our destruction is not imprisoned for spreading alarm and despondency, while the End-time preacher buys himself another Cadillac.

The prophet Jeremiah had a different experience. 'I have become a laughing stock all the day; everyone mocks me. For whenever I speak, I cry out, I shout "Violence and destruction!" ' ... 'Denounce him! Let us denounce him!' say all my familiar friends, watching for my fall'. He was not a happy man.

Now the emphasis has shifted. Those who don't believe in God do not fear Him, while those who do believe seem to have fallen into the sin of presumption. Perhaps despair is the worst sin, since it belittles the power of God, but presumption is most unwise since it seizes on the good news of redemption and ignores the uncomfortable fact that we still have responsibilities and cannot behave as we see fit without fear of retribution. We are dimly aware that we cannot keep all our Cadillacs and freezers full of goodies and have boundless electricity without something dire befalling us, but that's all someone else's fault. We've been brain-washed into believing that we have a right to be happy and can do what we like, and if what we like doing is not entirely consonant with the Commandments then that's probably someone else's fault too.

Jeremiah would not have got along with many of our senior clergymen. His God was no pussy cat. 'Like a lion he has left his covert.' The Lord of Hosts had threatened that 'those slain by the Lord on that day shall extend from one end of the earth to the other. They shall not be lamented or gathered or buried; they shall be dung on the surface of the ground.' There seems to be a perception that the Lord has calmed down since those days; but as we have the capability of destroying ourselves He doesn't need to throw His weight about. The saving and illuminating presence of Christ among us does not lessen but increases our responsibilities. Maybe a few unfashionable jeremiads would not come amiss. They'd make a bracing change from being patted on the head and exhorted to express ourselves.

21. THE TRUE CHURCH

A group of enthusiasts – modernists with bright new ideas – compiled a questionnaire asking whether the 'people' wished to see the Church reformed. Confidently they prepared themselves for the response, expecting a great demand for women priests, gay priests, or, ideally, no priests (there is a movement that wishes to see the priest replaced by a 'presider') and all the other breezy schemes that they had hatched up. They found the actual response disappointing: many people did want to see the Church reformed but not in the manner suggested. What they wanted was their Church *back*, the true Church not the new Church.

There is a great and understandable confusion both inside and outside, which is hardly surprising when you consider what's going on. The ordinary person in the pew often has little time or inclination to look into the state of catechetics and may not even be aware that his children are being fed heresy in school and his priest is talking a load of old guff. For instance, a cleric chatting about kiddies building sand castles, the glories of modern architecture and God doing a little dance for joy as he sees these things may sound unexceptionable, but behind it lies some dubious theology, carrying hints of the gnostic-inspired Creation Spirituality. Some bishops invite people to teach 'feminist, creation, political and liberation theology' in their diocese, but, as someone said, at the moment the only unacceptable heresy is orthodoxy, and anyone querying the value of these increasingly old-hat notions is firmly sat upon.

The madder feminism is still much in evidence with the goddess religion; white witches and high priestesses and occult notions are freely lavished on anyone daft enough to listen, together with a constant denigration of tradition and 'patriarchy'. An article in the excellent magazine *Christian Order* quotes the editor of the newsletter of the Catholic Women's Network of March 1997, relating the 'distress I felt at last year's Easter vigil because of the overtly sexual and violent way in which the priest had plunged the Pascal candle into the holy water.'

41

There is a Catholic priest who, it is alleged, has asked his congregation to sign a document disallowing the Church's teaching pre-Vatican II and at least one other who is a member of the Sea of Faith, a group which holds that God is a human construct. Some priests don't seem to believe in God at all, never mind the doctrines of the Faith, and one cannot imagine why they don't take up some other line of work.

There is a false ecumenism which requires us to put our brains in the cupboard under the stairs and embrace any old error for fear of giving offence. Attempts are made to clothe these errors in respectable garments: their adherents, when addressing the public at large, will contrive to appear almost sane. This adds to the confusion. We can't spend all our days lifting up sheepskins to discern the lunatic wolf beneath, and few of us would want to attend the events where the sheepskin is discarded and the animal appears in its true colours. A good deal of the 'new' thinking is derived from the propositions of Mme Blavatsky, who greatly influenced Nazi ideology. Evil can disguise itself as sheer silliness until we wake up and discover what a hold it has gained. True Christianity is notable for common sense, and when that goes out of the window we no longer have our religion but something quite else.

22. OPEN

⤜⟨⊹⟩⤛

There is a scene in films with which we must all be familiar: a door will not open, whereupon a person will charge it with his shoulder (which must be painful), revealing whatever has happened in the room beyond. A body will be discovered weltering in gore, or the window wide, curtains wafting in the breeze, a baffling silence. Sometimes it is still happening – an illicit game of chance or an adulterous liaison. I have nearly forgotten why I was thinking about this door, but it must be something to do with the Church and the difficulties encountered by the average parishioner with a question. In light-hearted films the door opens easily, leaving the hurtler looking silly on the floor, but in the more portentous dramas the door is stouter and the seeker after truth has to make several attempts and use considerable force before all is made plain.

After Vatican II and various other developments there was a general idea that everything was going to be much more *open*, and it was claimed that the windows of the Church would be flung wide to let in light and air. Should you force yourself in, chances are that all you will see is the curtain waving, while what you seek has disappeared. Sometimes, if you persevere, you will uncover a mouldering heresy (Pelagianism, Arianism for example) on to which someone has tried to impose a semblance of life but, should you collar a suspect, he will insist that no crime has been committed. Even caught red-handed the perpetrators will protest that they have been wilfully misunderstood and cruelly victimized.

Enough of that. In simple terms here are a few of the things the modernizers claim not to have done behind closed doors: diminished veneration of the Eucharist; attempted to sideline the Mother of God; discouraged homage to the saints; permitted travesties of doctrine to be taught in schools; reduced Mass attendance; lost vocations and irritated the faithful. Blandly or shrilly, they deny all charges and very often accuse the questioner of uncharitableness. They would, I suspect, like to accuse him of insolence and disobedience, too, but those words do not sound good spilling from the lips of liberals, and it is the liberals who have locked the door on enquiry. The dissenters will not tolerate dissent. Almost anything goes except critical scrutiny of their views, and they do not hesitate to attempt to silence those they perceive as their enemies, while extending a warm welcome to all manner of heretics and nutters. 'Ours is surely a religion of *love*,' they purr through gritted teeth when confrontation can no longer be deferred. 'What are you *afraid* of?' they ask sweetly when you catch them wrecking your heritage.

The answer is, of course, the Gates of Hell, but not a lot of them believe in that. The parish of Benalla in Australia was destroyed by a 'team ministry' of three modernist clerics backed by the local bishop, who did get cross enough to describe opponents of the move as 'malicious' and 'hateful', but, as a general rule, bishops prefer to keep the carnage under wraps and present a smooth, locked surface to the curious investigator.

It makes one quite nostalgic for the movies where the doors opened easily. There was always a body, but at least you knew where you were. The plot was simpler, the villain got his comeuppance and there was that satisfying moment when somebody explained everything. And there must have been far fewer actors with need of recourse to the chiropractor.

23. GENTEEL

The aptly named Cardinal Stickler has recently pointed out that the priest offers Mass in the person of Christ and not simply as president of a concelebrating assembly. This is why women cannot be priests; not *should* not but *cannot*. Just as men cannot be mothers: it all seems unfair to those who yearn to minimalize the difference between the sexes, but there it is. I have heard of a church in Scotland where a notice on the confessional reads Sister so and so, SND. There is no reason why people should not pour out their hearts to this sister, but she can't give them absolution. Therapy is now widely preferred to the awkward aspects of religion and a number of priests, as well as nuns, don't seem to believe in sin any more: they give you a metaphorical pat on the head, *de haut en bas*, and you have to make up your own penance. It is as though you had asked for bread and been given not even a stone but a handful of jelly babies. What they probably mean to present as compassion comes across as insulting goo.

Last time I went to confession the priest was determined to treat me as a victim. I've had a tough time – haven't we all? – but that's none of his business. If I want sympathy I'll ask for it, but I resent being treated as a receptacle for syrup, and several failures of communication arose during this episode. 'Oh, goody,' said the priest to himself (I may be doing him an injustice but that was the impression I got), 'here we have a lonely embittered widow who has not availed herself of the lovely new modernist insights of the present approach to religion. Let me remove her anxieties.'

So then we entered into a ludicrous exchange, with him suggesting my probable response to the vicissitudes I had encountered and me denying it. 'Christ was never angry,' says he at one point. 'Oh yes he was,' say I, correctly as it happens. I got quite exasperated myself, but not a hint of an overt rebuke came through the partition, only a wash of spurious understanding disguising a total lack of comprehension. I was trying to admit my sins and he was trying to commit social work on me. I was given no penance but told to go and sit down and let the peace of God take over. Unfortunately I could only think of smart things I should have said, but you can't go back in the box hissing, 'And what's more...'

A lot of people are determined to improve on the teachings of Christ where they feel they don't measure up to their own enlightened standards, but rather than say so they ignore or distort His words which leads to further confusion.

It seems that many of our 'theologians' are unfamiliar with the Bible, reading only commentaries and getting together for the purpose of mutual congratulation and propagation of heresy. It is all part of the grimly dangerous sentimentality, the new infantilism that pervades so many aspects of life today, while behind it evil flourishes, unacknowledged and unrebuked.

I have a feeling that if I'd confessed to serial murder the priest might have expressed concern about the well-being of my inner child. Once I would doubtless have been on the way to Hell. Only they don't believe in Hell any more. They are warmly tolerant of much shocking behaviour, but talk of retribution is considered indelicate. There is a perverse prudery, a genteelism in modern liberalism, and they don't think Hell is quite nice.

24. PASSIVE

❧ ✿ ❧

I came across an interesting malapropism in one of the papers a few weeks ago. A reviewer wrote of someone who was punished for 'passive concupiscence' in a bomb plot. Putting aside what this careless reviewer meant to say and concentrating on what the concept might imply is a taxing mental exercise.

We all know what passive smoking is supposed to do to the innocent bystander, but a deal of profound speculation has failed to give me a clear picture of the dangers inherent in passive concupiscence. I feel there must be some but cannot see what form they would take. Keeping copies of *Playboy* or *Cosmopolitan* under the pillow is too simple, and relatively harmless unless the reader is incited to violence. Perhaps I am being misled by the word 'passive' into trying to read too much into this slip of the pen. From long association with the awful word 'smoking', passive has come to have actively evil connotations. Concupiscence used to be frowned upon before sex was perceived as the greatest good, and passivity, while seldom acclaimed as a virtue, is now, I suspect, held in lower regard than slavering lust. The lust of the eyes, the lust of the flesh and the pride of life are probably considered by many to be a healthy means of self-expression. Before self-discipline was translated as repression people used to think twice before forcing their attentions on the person next to them. Come to think of it, the phrase 'self-discipline' now suggests only a sort of autonomous Miss Whiplash. Passive concupiscence perhaps?

Or could this new term be used in connection with the sex education programmes to which unsuspecting children are subjected? A recent report says that divorce has gone up by 600 per cent in 30 years, 200,000 mothers never see their children and 700,000 children never see their fathers. About 74,000 school children go to contraception clinics and last year 13,000 babies were born to girls under 16. The worse it gets the more eagerly do the savants hasten to offer ever more explicit sex instruction to ever younger children, and it gets worse again.

Children have always been inclined to mild sexual experiment but they weren't always told precisely how to do it: they were mostly told not to. Today about the only taboo words are 'Don't do that'. Could passive concupiscence be summed up as 'Those who can, do; those who can't, teach?'

At the other end of life people who should be concentrating on eschatological matters and gratefully accepting a certain degree of physical passivity are trying to turn the clock back by buying supplies of Viagra. One old gentleman, having obtained a bottle of these pills, telephoned his faithful elderly mistress and announced, 'I won't be coming home. It is time for me to become a stud again', and went off dancing. Several other old gentlemen have died of concupiscent enthusiasm – always a risk after a certain age.

I have given up trying to read meaning into passive concupiscence. Maybe it is just something the devil does in his spare time. Anyone got any ideas?

PS: The subject has suddenly taken on new life as I hear that the Church of England has a significant shareholding in the company that markets Viagra. It means that our reviewer has inadvertently hit on a phrase that could prove of inestimable value.

25. THE FLOCK AND THE SHEPHERD

Being tucked away in eremitic seclusion in the country means that I haven't seen a newspaper for some time, which is just as well in a way, since no self-respecting hermit would have the papers delivered and subject himself to the consternation and fruitless worry caused by the contents.

The TV offers only two channels and the radio spills forth either cricket or a crackle. Still, I did manage to hear that the Pope has at last had a stern word with the dissidents, and about time too. For too long those supposed to be in authority – our bishops and cardinals – have assured us blandly that there is really no rift in the Church, nothing of any significance anyway, and those who point out what is now a great gulf between orthodoxy and heterodoxy are told to shut up. People ask me how I feel when I have annoyed the Church leadership, and I am tired of explaining that it is not the Congregation for the Doctrine of the Faith which comes down on me like a ton of bricks but the *liberals and modernizers* who take umbrage when their enlightened notions and, more particularly, their motives are questioned. Some are merely weak and at the mercy of their advisors, and some are worse: those who are bent on destroying the Church. All of them cling grimly to what they perceive as the moral high ground and howl in outrage when not accorded the admiration they feel their position merits. Believe me, being pronounced anathema is as nothing compared to the earful you get from a liberal who considers himself insufficiently appreciated. They strenuously avoid the much vaunted 'debate' to which they claim they are committed and they don't answer letters. If they do, they restrict themselves to a few lines, assiduously avoiding the question and/or passing the buck, or give vent to extraordinarily childish spite.

I have seen a great deal of correspondence between the flock and the 'shepherds' and it is remarkable for the contrast in

49

approach and content. Letters from the flock tend to be long, expressing doubts about the current state of the liturgy, setting out questions in orderly progression and, on the whole, admirably restrained. The responses, when the shepherd bothers to respond at all, are short, inconsequential, frequently shrill and sometimes downright threatening. In the 'humanising' process, the individual expects to be loved for himself alone while insisting that the flock obeys his autonomous dictates. Priests and bishops urge the congregation to call them by their first names, but should you manage to get one on the telephone and ask, 'Tell me, Fred, where do you stand on transubstantiation? And what happened to the communion rails? And why do you permit the unauthorized person to handle the Host?', etc., he hangs up, offended.

I have never had a clear answer to questions about the demolition of the Faith and nor has anyone else I know. We are rejected with aggrieved dignity, bad temper or a soothing burble. 'Don't rock the boat', says the crew, as it breaks up, pieces of it drifting away in opposite directions. The various dissenting movements, such as the toe-curling 'We are Church', should be cut adrift and left to their own devices, not encouraged to drown the rest of us. The humanist protestantism to which the liberals incline is a first dip in the sea of atheism, and it's cold out there. It is high time the Pope put out a call for the ship's carpenter.

26. ORDINATION OF WOMEN

In answer to correspondents' queries: the initials SND stand for Sisters of Notre Dame, although some wags now suggest that Sisters of No Discipline is more apposite. Certainly their founder Julie Billiart of Namur would find it hard to recognize her Community as they run around in the unbecoming modernized clothing they have chosen for themselves. There are fewer of them now and while I'm sure some are as good as gold there are others with whom you would not wish to spend time: feminists and advocates of the ordination of women, which brings me to another query. Why can't women be priests? In answer to this I can do no better than recommend a new book, *The Inner Goddess*, by Josephine Robinson (Gracewing, £7.99). To begin with, she explains, Christ was male and so were the apostles. Feminists suggest that this was because of the society and the time in which He lived, but as He was not noticeably constrained by other contemporary rules and modes of decorum the argument does not stand up. It seems a little impudent to claim that God was too old-fashioned and short-sighted to choose women as his apostles. He had many female friends and it was the Magdalen to whom He first appeared after the Resurrection, but it was of Peter that He said 'Upon this rock I will build my church' and it was the apostles to whom He addressed himself at the Last Supper. Of course if God is removed from religion, as seems to be the aim of many, then anyone can be a priest just as anyone can claim to be a theologian without apparently having done any homework. The urge to cram the whole subject into a form compatible with all human desires and inclinations causes the point to be lost. St John of the Cross wrote 'Many…want God to desire what they want, and become sad if they have to desire God's will…hence they frequently believe that what is not their will, or that which brings them no satisfaction is not God's will. They measure God by themselves and not themselves by God.'

Advocates of the ordination of women and homosexuals are

starting from a new premise, leaving the past out of account. This is often known as 'development of doctrine' and allows for much individual interpretation. If Tony Blair on his hols reads St Augustine's *Confessions*, a copy of which was given to him by a priest, he will find the following: 'Therefore shameful acts which are contrary to nature, such as the acts of the Sodomites, are everywhere and always to be detested and punished. Even if all people should do them, they would be liable to the same condemnation by divine law; for it has not made men to use one another in this way. Indeed the social bond which should exist between God and us is violated when the nature of which He is the author is polluted by a perversion of sexual desire'. This is why the much vaunted Debate is a waste of time. No one sharing the above opinion will find much in common with Bishop Spong or Peter Tatchell, not if they sit round a table talking till the crack of doom. The wistful yearning of the Church of England for an inclusive, homogeneous organization beaming forth sweetness and light is dependent on silence, on the old dinner-party conversational rule: no mention of sex, religion, politics or money. Just praise the flower arrangement and don't blow your nose on the napkin. Keep quiet and all will be well. Only it won't.

27. A CROSS LIBERAL

As I have observed before, a liberal crossed is a cross liberal. He cannot believe his ears when his views are questioned, and he reacts with a self-righteousness unparalleled by the most fervent religious fundamentalist. This was apparent when Islam took exception to *The Satanic Verses*. Regarding censorship as far worse than blasphemy, the liberals were unable to grasp the depth of feeling behind the furore and made for the moral high ground as creatures fleeing a flash flood will spring up the nearest tree. The same reaction was evident after the latest Church of England Synod when the African and Asian bishops voted overwhelmingly against the ordination of active homosexuals. One disgruntled liberal cleric remarked memorably that this was 'blackmail'. It must be peculiarly disturbing for them when there is a clash between the causes dearest to their hearts.

Some years ago when I politely pointed out in an article in a Catholic paper that under the late Archbishop of Liverpool, God rest his soul, Mass attendance and vocations had sunk to unprecedented levels, it was not the Vatican that demanded I be suppressed but the liberal wing of the Church. It was the doughty defenders of free speech who insisted I be sacked.

A recent article in the *Sunday Times* takes issue with the Vatican on the subject of the censorship of liberal views, which is ironic when you consider the amount of heretical piffle that our bishops permit to be circulated in their dioceses. The writer waxes indignant over the case of Sister Lavinia Byrne who 'teaches religious journalism to ordinands in Cambridge' and has written a book called *Woman at the Altar*, modestly advocating ordination for women and apparently stating that the invention of the contraceptive pill was 'a milestone in women's liberation'. He tells us that Sister Lavinia 'took the veil aged 17'. I wonder what she did with it – the only time I met her she was wearing an orange jumper and pearl earrings. I haven't read *Woman at the Altar* but I have read one about notable females compiled by Sister Lavinia. On my shelves I have a number of works by Victorian authors entitled *Heroines of History, Stories of the Lives of Noble Women*, etc, etc. They are there as curiosities, mostly for their comic value, and Sister Lavinia's book could join them without adding a jarring note. It is unencumbered by historical or psychological complexity, merely seeking to prove that women are a good thing by giving examples.

Sister Lavinia is very upset about the Church's treatment of witches, failing to mention that Luther held that witches should be burnt even if they did no harm – merely for making a pact with the devil – and it was Calvin who announced that 'the Bible teaches us that there are witches and that they must be slain'. There was a witch madness abroad in the 16th century. It was a savage time, and the Church was infected along with everyone else.

It seems that Sister Lavinia's *Woman at the Altar* has not met with Vatican approval and that she is 'horrified by this brutal act of censorship' while 'as a human being' she feels 'bullied'. Oh, for goodness sake! It is high time that the Vatican did something about the numerous fads and fancies that bedevil the Church. I'm sure Sister Lavinia is a nice enough woman, but the suppression of her book will not represent a great loss to literature or theology, and if she is bewildered by the failure of the orthodox Catholic to appreciate it then she can't be thinking too clearly. One of the duties of the Vatican is to preserve the faithful from erroneous doctrine, not to turn a blind eye.

28. SNIGGERING

Political correctness has been hard on the entertainment industry, especially the comic branch. They can't be rude about Jews, they daren't sauce the Muslims, they are oddly respectful towards Buddhism, probably because they don't understand it, the Hindu caste system baffles even the most sardonic performer, mothers-in-law and blacks are protected species, so what's left apart from Mr Clinton? Christianity of course, and Catholicism in particular. Here the comedian can be as daring and frightfully naughty as he likes with no fear of the consequences (hell-fire aside, but that's another matter). He can be cheeky to teacher, flip chalk and snigger in the back row to his heart's content. There is obviously no point in picking on aspects of the new church that are funny already – lesbian nuns, circle dancing, goddess worship, guitars, strange rites that priests and congregations invent together, heresies and hysterical trances, etc. – so the comedian attacks, with what I suppose he imagines to be biting satire, a church that never in fact existed: an austere, humourless organization run by bigots and sadists. I think he must have been influenced by the modernists and the progressives in whose interests it is to denigrate that which they seek to destroy. Even comedians seem to be sadly gullible.

Then we have the earnest commentators dripping compassion for the people who are out of favour with the Vatican. The 'mild-mannered', the 'bewildered', the 'truth-seeking' who, they imply, wouldn't say boo to a goose but are simply doing their best. I'm reminded of that sweet, fluffy little object in the long grass that turns out to be the tip of the tail of the sabre-toothed tiger. These people are threatening in their various ways. As long, that is, as you regard the loss of souls as a matter for regret.

Take Fr Tisa Balasuiriya upon whom so much tender pity has been squandered. His views on more or less everything are at odds with Catholic orthodoxy, and his admirers are the madder New Agers and feminists. He said, 'A Lenin or a Mao Tse-Tung cannot be fully appreciated without seeing the mystical traits of their struggles ... the lifestyle of Ho Chi Minh was as attractive in its simplicity and as daring as those of great religious liberators.' I think I heard him on the radio explaining that in his church he had a line of statues of Jesus and Buddha and other notable figures (I'm not sure that Kali wasn't one of them, but I may have imagined that) and, as far as I can tell, the people were invited to do pujas to whichever one they fancied. The man can't behave like that and still hope to be considered a Catholic priest.

If a confectioner abandoned the sale of chocolate bars and bullseyes and took to selling lamb chops and ribs of beef, he would be expected to change the sign over his door. There is a move to make Christianity resemble the food on offer in American supermarkets: fat-free, salt-free, sugar-free and so bland that many commodities are indistinguishable from each other. Any taste that remains has been introduced in the form of additives since real food is regarded as somehow dangerous. The human race must be given only the minced, the pasteurized, the processed and the de-natured until all their souls are as flabby as their bodies and it isn't really funny at all.

29. LYING

If I had been the parent of a child who, at an early age, had come to me and said, 'Father, I cannot tell a lie', and had gone on to confess that it was he, with his little axe, who had chopped down that cherry tree, I would have rolled up my eyes and gone to my wife and said, 'Honey, it's no good. The kid'll never make a politician. Put him down for lumberjack school'. Lying is loathsome, certainly, and leads to all manner of confusion which we could well do without, but it is understandable and a sign of intelligence: naughty, distorted intelligence, maybe, but evidence of the action of thought, and, at its least harmful, an effort at self-preservation. Telling lies about others, spreading slanders and making trouble is another matter, and can never be condoned.

All right, lying should never be condoned, but you can see the point when retribution looms. The phrase, 'OK, Guv, you got me bang to rights', is seldom uttered in reality, not immediately anyway. Later, when the liar has been exposed, it is doubtless often a relief, not only to the conscience but also to the brain cells, to give up the struggle and tell the simple truth. To get away with a lie you need a phenomenal memory and the combined skills of a Senior Wrangler and a Shakespearean actor. What is odder is the ever-more-prevalent compulsion not to deny wrongdoing but to claim you couldn't help it: the Ron Davies line that we are what we are and it's all the fault of our genes and our early experience and we cannot really be held responsible at all. It's rather like claiming that we don't really exist, for if we have no free will we are puppets.

Luther shared this cast of thought. In a sermon in 1524 he said, 'I have often attempted to become good, however, the more I struggle, the less I succeed. Behold then what free will is'. So he gave up, claiming that the human will was like a horse with God or the devil in the saddle, and that was that. Man 'has no power to run to one or the other of the two riders and offer himself to him, but the riders fight to obtain possession of the animal'. So, as Heinrich Denifle observed, Luther 'became the spokesman of that society whose supreme principle was that natural instinct cannot be resisted, that it must be satisfied.'

It sounds sadly familiar. There are few new heresies, just the old ones dressed up. If it's not God or the devil driving us, then it's our genes, and we cannot be held culpable – the doctrine of the enslaved will. Whenever Luther did something of which he doubted the propriety, he blamed God, seeming not to entertain the possibility – put forward by himself – that he had the devil on his back. He even used the dreadful excuse, 'I was only obeying orders.' Of his complicity in murder he wrote, 'I, Martin Luther, have slain all the peasants at the time of their rebellion, for I commanded them to be killed; their blood is upon me. But I cast it upon our Lord God; He commanded me to speak as I did.'

The notion of the enslaved will appeals only to the scoundrel, the coward, or the feeble of intellect. The road to hell must ring with the cry, 'It wasn't my fault!' Unless, of course, God in His infinite mercy has pointed out to the protesters the error of their ways and reminded them that He has paid His creation the extraordinary compliment of giving us freedom of choice.

30. A BAD JOKE

The other day, on the radio, somebody spoke of a female artist who worked in the Fifties. She had painted something – or maybe just said something – sexually explicit and this was absolutely unheard of in those days. What a daring and original girl, was the implication. I was at art school in the Fifties and, to the best of my recollection, nobody ever talked about anything much except sex, while the more earnest students drew erotic pictures, threw erotic pots and wove erotic motifs into table mats. They went around with copies of D H Lawrence tucked under their arms and took the whole subject very seriously. Some took it light-heartedly, but they were the exception.

Outside the art school it was different. A friend who was aiming for a career in politics (Old Labour) meanwhile worked part-time in a factory. The female workers spent their days teasing the male apprentices with dreadful stories of the risks implicit in the wrong choice of girlfriend; something to do with screws and left- and right-handed threads. In the horsey set, there was a joke about the girl at the Hunt Ball who remembered to bring her undies but not her ovaries. It was considered a real hoot. Older people had more discretion and understood that some jokes could be told before the assembled house party but others only individually behind the potted palms. People sent seaside postcards but obscenity was not all-pervasive. No one had latched on to the advertising possibilities of sex and they had other things to think about. Rationing for one, and there wasn't much money around.

They laughed about religion too. A famous series of cartoons by Hugh Burnett was set in monasteries, but they seldom descended into blasphemy. Left-wing intellectuals preferred to try arguing you out of your faith rather than to simply raise a laugh. They were well-educated and, even if they thought you mad, knew more or less what was meant by tran-substantiation and eschatology. Now many people are virtually uneducated, particularly in historical matters, and most religious education is a bad joke in itself. The overall coarsening of society is the result of ignorance. A supermarket chain advertized something with a picture of two chefs beside a baptismal font filled with goodies: one held a chalice and one a thurible. Their response to complaints was, 'All I can say is that if it has caused any offence to anybody we are deeply sorry and would like to give our apologies.' They hadn't thought there was anything peculiar about this image and were innocent of malice. Just dumb.

I saw an Advent calendar with a skeleton on the front and a 'Spooky Surprise Behind Every Window' ('Why do mummies make good employees? – They're all wrapped up in their work'). Another was inspired by *The Terminator*. On the back was the mask of a frightful brute with a flat head. 'ASK AN ADULT TO HELP YOU CUT AROUND THE OUTSIDE BLACK LINE WITH A PAIR OF ROUND-HEADED SCISSORS.' This at least seems to acknowledge that anyone stupid enough to buy it should not be trusted with anything sharp. It has chocolates in each window, doubtless to help the kiddies through the Advent fast.

A child at a supposedly Catholic school was puzzled by this year's Nativity play: Mary and Joseph strolled onto the stage and sat down, remaining silent throughout while everyone else made like a snowflake. 'And that's it?' I asked. 'That's it.' I suppose they were thinking 'Winterval' rather than Christmas, since now the only real solecism is to be a Christian.

31. WANTED:
AN INTELLIGENT ATHEIST

I don't know whom I'd choose if I was told I had to spend eternity, or even a brief train journey, with either an atheist or a preacher. I wouldn't mind a subtle and informed theologian, but there are very few of those around at the moment: the ones we have lean towards either atheism or dissent, and have the same tendency to drone on. Sometimes the atheist seems the more irritating, assuming as he does that the believer is unacquainted with doubt and has never questioned his own beliefs: he will look at you with the feigned amusement of the humourless, and enquire cunningly whether you have ever seen or touched God. When you say that no, you have not, he will point a finger at you in triumph and claim a victory. It is fruitless for the believer to explain that he has been everywhere the atheist has been and gone further. As far as the atheist is concerned there is no further. He's got as far as the end of his nose and there he stays. While this may seem like an oversimplification, actually it isn't.

Then there are the Bible-thumpers, those whose regard for the Good Book approaches idolatry and whom George Melly categorized as 'God-botherers'. In America, as you turn the knob on the wireless in a vain search for the World Service, you will keep coming up against preachers, apparently tireless beings with an inexhaustible stock of biblical quotations. Like the atheist, the preacher is given to triumphant exclamations, but in this case there usually follows a rendition of a verse in Isaiah or something Jeremiah said in one of his moods. Having enunciated these words, the preacher seems to think that there is nothing more to be said on the matter, whatever the matter may be. One of them suggests that the Bible is an aid to slimming: you read a passage and then go for a walk to mull it over in your mind. Weight loss will inevitably result. You almost find yourself wishing that Wycliffe had turned his energies in another direction. Between recitations the preachers will insist that we immediately strike up a personal relationship with the Lord Jesus Christ or go to hell. They do not explain how this instant fix is to be achieved. As far as I can tell it's a *feeling*, and good works get you nowhere.

President Clinton, I have been told, as a born-again Baptist, believes his salvation to be assured no matter what sins he commits. Perhaps this will be of some comfort to the poor wretch as he faces trial for 'high crimes and misdemeanors'. The President has said, reasonably enough, that his problems were between himself, his family and 'our God'. Less reasonably, he appears to think that sexual behaviour which stops short of penetration does not constitute adultery. He believes in freedom of conscience, 'soul competency', the priesthood of all believers, the privilege of direct access to God without a human intermediary and the ability of a 'Spirit-led' Christian to interpret the Bible all by himself. Some of his fellow-Baptists have pointed out that this is all very fine and large, but does not give him licence to work out 'personal rules'. I don't really see why not when it's every man for himself and whatever he does he cannot lose his salvation.

Most of the more vociferous preachers also adhere to the views of Mr Clinton and imagine that since there is nothing more to be said, their listeners will find it interesting to hear the proposition constantly reiterated without any tiresome digression into what might be perceived as profundity. The dark night of the soul is not a subject that they care to address. Perhaps on the whole an intelligent atheist, if that's not an oxymoron, might be preferable company.

32. FLUFFY-MINDEDNESS

A number of subtle transactions lie at the heart of the more ancient forms of Christianity: the requirement that we should see Christ in the leper and the beggar and behave accordingly; the need to forgive in order to be forgiven; the constant exercise of charity in all its forms, not simply for the sake of others, nor for our own, but to make ourselves more pleasing in the eyes of God. One would, after all, prefer to offer one's best beloved a nice fresh bunch of flowers rather than a clump of withering, decaying old weeds.

All this is now out of style. Locating God within ourselves is not the same as seeing Christ in others; the PC attitude of understanding – and hence abandoning – any notion of sin is not the same as forgiveness; the concept of charity is seen as patronising and has largely disappeared under an ever-increasing heap of 'rights'; and the worship of God is eroded by the fluffy-minded who would reduce religion to humanism with bells on. No, not bells. They don't like bells. Let's just say humanism and be done with it. Küng, feminists, Boff, Balasuriya, as well as a whole lot of other people who should know better, don't care for the idea of authority or hierarchy and demand 'democracy', as if that had ever had anything to do with religion. The voice of the People is usually raised only when they want their own way and can't be bothered with all those tiresome sanctions. *Vox populi* is not *vox Dei*, not by a long chalk. Not under any circumstances.

The mix of greed and sentimentality, backed by near total ignorance of theology or Church history, that emanates from the modernist mob is frightening and repulsive – and ubiquitous. The recent TV production *Absolute Truth*, which purported to examine the state of the Catholic Church, was yet another dreary re-run of the views of the dissenters, embellished every now and then with pleas for the wider use of condoms. A radio 'comedian' doing a pub sketch says something along the lines of 'He took bread in his holy and venerable hands and produced a ploughman's lunch', a priest in his homily announces he has been reading a book of such profound spirituality that it nearly made him cry. What can this be? wonders the congregation. St John of the Cross? *The History of the Soul* of St Thérèse? Some newly discovered poem by Gerard Manley Hopkins? No. The priest has been reading *Jonathan Livingston Seagull*. Oh God. Faced with all this debilitating piffle (not to mention the priests in Brazil who, it seems, perform aerobics in the sanctuary and go clubbing in order to endear themselves to the parishioners), one is understandably inclined to seek relief elsewhere.

Atheism is not the answer. Atheists are quite as silly as everyone else and more conceited than anyone. Their impregnable vanity is a bar to communication and they seldom have a sense of humour. Take Ludovic Kennedy, who seems to find in Walter Savage Landor and the bagpipes a substitute for religion. He dances reels and strathspeys to the 'beat of pipe music' and tells us so. I thought nothing could be more bizarre than the priest and congregation dancing round the altar, but the thought of the old atheist capering about in a kilt is engagingly daft. He doesn't find it funny in the least. I'm going out to look at the sheep and forget all about my own species for a while.

33. NUT CUTLETS

'Nature I loved and next to Nature, Art: I warmed both hands before the fire of Life; It sinks and I am ready to depart.' This Dying Speech of an Old Philosopher, much admired by Ludovic Kennedy, is to the atheist as the nut cutlet to the vegetarian. Denying the need for God/meat, they yet offer substitutes. There is something so annoying in these lines that one wishes one could have been present at the deathbed of Landor to see just how ready he was as the shades of night closed in. He begins, 'I strove with none for none was worth my Strife'; which is even more irritating. Who does he think he is – was – one asks oneself, and did he never have a cross word with anyone?

Observing the atheist and the vegetarian posturing on the moral high ground one cannot but hope to see them fall off. (There was a certain amount of glee when it was learned that George Bernard Shaw, who disapproved of eating animals, needed injections of liver extract or something to correct a tendency to anaemia. He should have relied more on the lentil, but that's beside the point.) We used to be accustomed to our religious exponents telling us what was what: that was their purpose whether we liked it or not. It was what they were paid to do. Now most of them are too nervous to mention their beliefs – if they've even got them any more – and subject us instead to anodyne twaddle about their own experience with, as often as not, a few naughty words to convince us of their humanity. (I will not soon forget Lionel Blue on the Ten Commandments, speaking of coveting his neighbour's ass and telling us coyly that that was something he'd never do.) Ministers of both sexes confide in us their family problems or describe the cutely insightful remarks the kiddies made on the deeper significance of the Resurrection as they curled up to go to sleep.

One begins to long for a good knock-down, drag 'em out sermon on Hell Fire and Damnation. Rather as the vegetarian yearns sometimes for a steak, perhaps. Now all we have is the likes of Richard Dawkins taking over the sternly didactic tone and telling us that instilling religious belief in children is akin to child abuse. (Children need proper religious instruction or they get their own cute ideas and their parents quote them.)

Does some bishop leap to refute this? No he doesn't. He's probably too busy already, overseeing the watering down of religious instruction in his diocese until it attains the degree of blandness that will offend no one. I lived through one age of atheism/vegetarianism and high-minded humanism, with whiskers, sandals and amber beads, and it was tedious then. Seeing it come up on the dreary wheel yet again is almost more than I can bear. I've heard it all before.

Listening to the Libby Purves show, I was struck by the apparent urgent necessity to denigrate the old type of religious sister. Two people spoke rather warmly of their experience of convents and nuns and then – was there a signal? a nudge in the ribs? a reminder of some injunction against speaking nicely of nuns? – they added hastily that, of course, some of them had been really cruel.

There is something Satanic in the current misrepresentations of Christianity, the distortion of the past, the dismissal of ancient goodness, the sneering and the mirth, the determination to twist history to fit the purposes of the ideologue, the lying, the substitution of 'humanist values'. But putting aside the evil inherent in all of this, what is most striking is that it is so bloody *boring*. I hate nut cutlets.

34. TRUTH IS BEAUTY

As Arthur Machen observed, '"Spiritual" does not mean "respectable", it does not even mean "moral", it does not mean "good" in the ordinary acceptation of the word. It signifies the royal prerogative of man, differentiating him from the beasts.' The atheist is uneasy with this idea: it strikes him as irrational and, while he must know that man differs from the ape and the dog in certain respects, he sees it mostly as a matter of degree.

One of the extraordinary things about atheists is their conviction that their point of view comes as a great surprise to the theist. 'Come on', they scoff. 'You can't believe all that stuff about the Virgin Birth and the Resurrection.' To which the answer is – I've thought about it and no I can't, but I do. This response arises, not from stubborn stupidity or a failure to listen to the arguments, but from an awareness of our lack of understanding, combined with a sense of something just beyond the borders of consciousness, just out of reach but not to be denied. Refusal to contemplate this *something* leads not to peace of mind but to a sort of irritable confusion. I had a friend, a noted atheist, who, after an argument, made me think of a savage dancing triumphantly round a tree treading on the supposed bones of his enemy, while the said enemy perched in the branches gazing down with a puzzled expression. There is no common ground and no point in sitting down round that table, so dear to the rationalist, to 'talk it out'.

We do have a lot in common with the beasts, but I'm conscious of the difference between us. We're not as shocked at the behaviour of the dog as we are by that of our politicians, unless, of course, we take the view that their antics are the result of being 'only human', in which case they can't be held to blame, being, after all, so closely related to the ape and the dog. It is usually the more or less innocent who feel guilt, those who have not stamped out all sparks of conscience, while the mildly culpable who adhere to the notion of 'human nature', the ones caught in other people's bedrooms or fiddling the till, are usually only cross at being found out. The truly wicked often wear an air of serenity, generally associated in the popular mind with the attainment of high virtue. There is a dark side to spirituality which leads to more evil than the mere animal aspects of our natures. The disobedient Lucifer was once the brightest angel in heaven. If he had been a dog he would doubtless have come to heel. As it was he took the form of a serpent – a strangely intractable and alien creature.

It all began in the Garden with the eating of the fruit of the Tree of Knowledge of Good and Evil. We fell out with both the animals and the angels and effectively isolated ourselves. The saddest, most mysterious part of this story is that we lost so much and learned so little. God left us with our souls but no longer comes to walk with us in the cool of the evening. We have a sense of loss which some seek to assuage by getting back to nature, which can be dangerous; some by worship of art, which is idolatrous; and some by denying that they're aware of any lack at all, which is nice for them. The worst take on themselves the power over life and death.

Still, art does have its consolations. I quote some words which have given me more comfort than the works of W S Landor: 'I wish I liked the human race, I wish I liked its silly face, I wish I liked the way it walks, I wish I liked the way it talks, And when I'm introduced to one, I wish I thought what jolly fun.' Keats remarked that truth is beauty, and I find that very beautiful.

35. GOODNESS, HOLINESS

Goodness is out of style; selflessness and humility are seen not as virtues but as character defects and those who discern tendencies towards these traits in themselves are wont to seek medical advice, fearing that they lack self-esteem – that attribute which appears, at present, to be regarded as the highest good. The meaning of the word *good* is now obscure. Manifestations of goodness in the old-fashioned or religious sense are treated not only with suspicion but in some cases with downright loathing: this is not due to the commendable vigilance which looks for signs of hypocrisy in the saint, but to detestation of his qualities and to what would once have been described as hatred of holiness – a demonic response.

The democratic distaste for elitism has extended as far as the spiritual realm and we like our heroes flawed, since then they offer us no reproach. The strange human compulsion to prefer the ersatz to the real is now in evidence and is somehow related to our fear of mortality. Highly coloured sentimentality is a more comforting response to death than acceptance of the stark facts and it was easier to mourn the demise of the Princess of Wales than contemplate the life of Mother Teresa, which might have caused us to examine our consciences. There were many attempts to discredit the old nun but it was a brave man who, at the time, said a word in disfavour of the Princess. Rather absurdly she was seen as 'one of us', while the peasant Mother Teresa was beyond the comprehension of most people and largely disregarded in the secular world. Christopher Hitchens has attempted to do a hatchet job on her but missed the mark. He must, however, be forgiven much for descrying in Diana the lineaments of Madeleine Bassett.

Now Padre Pio is the focus of incomprehension and hostility. He was loved and sought after in his lifetime, but his superiors regarded what threatened to become his cult with prudent reserve. The Church, contrary to popular opinion, has always been wary of its saints and properly alert to the possibility of charlatanism. His beatification has brought him back under the spotlight and most commentators have been unable to concentrate on any aspect of his life apart from his stigmata and the rumour that he was one for the ladies. The possibility that he was a truly good and holy man is too uncomfortable to contemplate at a time when self-conceit and greed are accepted with placid equanimity. I'm thinking of those numerous TV ads which celebrate a sort of solipsistic gluttony, with people gobbling up the last scrap of various brands of chocolate while congratulating themselves on not sharing it with their nearest and dearest.

If this is regarded as the norm and something to emulate then it's no wonder that the cardinal virtues are held in contempt. The English have never – at least since the Reformation – felt at ease with people who put God first. A book for children published in 1856 contains the following: 'I wish, my dear mother, that you had seen the friar: you would have been charmed with the sanctity and the innocence of his life'. Mother responds, 'I admire his good intentions but condemn the principle that misleads him to suppose that a life of indolent retirement is more acceptable to the Deity than an active course of usefulness in society'. No matter that this earlier Capuchin rose in the dark and spent all his time praying on his knees, working in the fields or hearing confessions. Goodness, holiness were suspect then and they're suspect now.

36. ETERNITY ON A
CRUISE LINER

A common liberal failing is the urge to pretend that human nature is as the liberal would like and thinks it should be, which is still about as practical as trying to make a silk purse out of a sow's ear. No matter how elevated the vision, without the appropriate materials, it can only remain a vision. The consequences of the pretence are unfortunate, since the visionary is not dealing in reality and hence can have no real effect, can bring about no actual changes but only persuade the masses to share in the fiction, which makes them complacent and gives the visionary a vastly inflated conceit of himself.

The Blairite insistence on the concern of the British people for the people of the Balkans is a case in point. Some, usually those who have witnessed the horrors at first hand, care deeply, but most are indifferent, although few would admit it except behind closed doors. Rex Stout in a Nero Wolfe novel of 1940 has a Montenegrin girl ask, 'It's too complicated for you, the Balkans' history?' to which Archie Goodwin responds with commendable candour, 'I don't know, I haven't tried it. But I understand all the kings and queens got murdered. I like newspaper murders better.' There's an old story about two people out walking when one remarks, 'There are 57 cows in that field', and the other goes cold because the human brain doesn't work that way and the most the eye can compute at a glance is five. No more can the human heart truly love more than a handful of people. Swift, another candid fellow, wrote in a letter, 'Principally I hate and detest that animal called man: although I heartily love John, Peter, Thomas and so forth.'

In all the periodic outbreaks of emotion over the death of some public figure only a few brave souls dare say they don't give a damn and retain the right to grieve only over the loss of their nearest and dearest. The honest, human response is greeted with shocked disapproval, and the display of mass hysteria, easy sentimentality and a hypocrisy so deeply entrenched that it is indiscernible on casual examination is the currency of our times. We would be doing ourselves less than justice if we failed to express ourselves in lamentation and tears and the distribution of 'floral tributes.'

An unwittingly comical cleric on the radio told his congregation that there were a good few hundred of them present and they'd do well to remember that it was going to be like that in heaven. It came across as an awful threat, a sentence to eternity on a cruise liner with the implication that there would be plenty of fellow-passengers they would not get along with but they'd bloody well better, or else. It sounded more like Sartre's idea of hell – other people – than an infinity of bliss. The preacher's tones were revealingly gloomy: he was not leaping about with joy at the prospect but obviously felt he must concur in the current notion that we are all as one, good, bad and indifferent, and should somehow contrive to be pleased about it.

It would be a reckless preacher or politician who delivered the old-fashioned type of homily that we are a pretty deplorable lot on the whole and should make some attempt at self-improvement. This would not reflect well on the speaker in our democratic times, since he would think it invidious to distinguish himself from his listeners, and then again he might lose his following by uttering some unwelcome truths. With a cavalier disregard for the evidence he intimates that we are all good, we all love each other really and we are all saved. No problem. Sweet dreams.

37. GROUNDWEED

There are still people around who were at their most impressionable in the Sixties. In most cases it doesn't matter much; they provide a source of mild general amusement and are a slight embarrassment to their families, but they don't trouble the rest of us unduly. It's different when they hold positions of influence, and some schools, architects' offices and churches are even now afflicted by the blight.

Certain priests in particular seem unable to shake themselves free of ideas that were old hat at the time, and persist in moving the furniture around to the intense irritation of the parishioners. One delivered himself recently of the pastoral observation that people who don't like it could 'take a hike'; others who raise the ire of the congregation whinge that failure to understand their moves is very wounding to them personally and inconsistent with Christianity. Remember charity and tolerance, they whine as they hack out the altar rails or bring in a circle of stacking chairs and make space for a guitarist. In their parish letters they dither between appeal and bossiness, making it clear that they're going to get their way come hell or high water and implying at the same time that Jesus would never have been so mean to them as the old person who just enquired where it was that they'd tucked away the Blessed Sacrament.

This is peculiarly maddening, the tactic of the bully confronted who blusters that he's going to tell his mother who's bigger than yours, or that he's going to lay the matter before the headmaster. An Irish Archbishop, intent on 're-ordering' a cathedral, recently sought Cardinal Ratzinger's reassurance that the destruction was mandatory, only to be told that it was not – 'such changes, while inspired by liturgical reform, cannot however be said to be *required* by the legislation of the Church.' Nothing daunted, the Archbishop removed the altar rails, had concrete poured on the mosaic floor, took away the pulpit and contrived to obscure the stained-glass East window, announcing that, 'We are all a part of a living, evolving Church and a living, evolving liturgy', and what that has to do with the desecration of the cathedral is anybody's guess. The ageing flower-children would doubtless claim it gives a more ecumenical feel to the place, makes it seem less authoritarian, more in keeping with the spirit of the times – in other words, ugly, barren, direction-less and devoid of spirituality. Their attempt at 'renewal', far from encouraging unity of the churches, has succeeded only in alien-ating vast numbers of the faithful. They seem unaware that 'Modernism' is, by definition, already dated – Formica, nylon, high-rise blocks, candles in Chianti bottles and the 'Spirit of Vatican II'.

Meanwhile the Protestants... A vicar has seen fit to organize an exhibition of pictures, one of which shows Christ crucified flanked by two pigs' heads. He says he hopes it will make people ask questions. I'm sure it will, the most usual, I imagine, being 'What the – is that?' But it is not the risible trendiness of these clerics that gives cause for alarm. The parish letter of an inner London RC church quotes the following remarkable lines: 'You have died with Christ and are set free from the ruling spirits of the universe. *Col.* ii 20.' I have gone through my various bibles and failed to track down this reading. It sounds like Manicheism, the heresy that St Thomas Aquinas demolished some time past, but heresy is like groundweed and hard enough to eradicate with-out the gardeners encouraging it to flourish.

38. 'ME'

The utilitarian 'what's in it for me?' approach to religion is self-defeating and the search for 'inner peace' can be as much grounded in greed as the quest for wealth.

In 1854, one James Hamilton, addressing the Kirk Session and Congregation of the National Scotch Church, Regent Square, wrote that some people 'fancy that there is no outlet for piety except in emotion. They forget that the engine may be doing most work when none of the steam is blowing off, and therefore they are not content except they *feel* a great deal and live in constant excitement... or they have just been singing, under some extraordinary afflatus, a hymn about universal peace or millennial glory; but the unopened letter turns out to be from some nefarious correspondent, or the moment the worship is over some gross negligence or some provoking carelessness accosts them, and the instant explosion proves that were they living in the millennium, there would be at least one exception to the universal peace.'

One gets the unmistakable impression that he had personal experience of members of the congregation, carried away by enthusiasm, behaving in a manner familiar to us today. A recent TV programme concerned with what was described as the 'spiritual revival' of the Sixties showed various people who had chosen to take up witchcraft, become devotees of Krishna, or the Guru Maharishi-ji (a portly 15-year-old), or the one I can only remember as the Bagwash, or a man who directed prayers into a box and pointed it at mountains. All of them, as far as I could gather, were avowedly dedicated to bringing about world peace or were awaiting the imminent arrival of some uniquely Superior Being who would make everything all right, here and now.

None of them seemed unduly perturbed by the non-materialization of their hopes, but explained that their fulfilment was merely postponed – something which travellers by public transport are accustomed to and might be expected to take in their stride – while the people with the box assured us that only by its efficacy had a Third World War been averted.

It was all great fun, but it must be admitted that the person who appeared actively maddest was the vicar engaged in exorcising a man who had dedicated himself to witchcraft. He shook himself about like a herring on a griddle. All those involved would doubtless claim that they had the good of the majority at heart, but the conclusion was inescapable that what they sought was self-satisfaction. Nor can it be claimed that excess is the province only of the lunatic fringe: Christianity has always had its Holy Rollers, and they are still around, dancing in circles, falling over 'slain in the spirit' or babbling in 'tongues.'

It would be pleasant to think that the trend was fading and common sense and true charity were being reasserted but there isn't much evidence of that. The insistence that 'liberal' values prevail and anything goes gets in the way of reality, and the populace, appalled by what it would rather not see, turns to fantasy and alterations of consciousness in the quest for 'enlightenment', which means, too often, escape from the horrid actuality of earthly existence and the need to do anything about it. Personal commitment to the good of others, unless there is some credit to be gained, is out of style and 'Me' reigns, frequently alone in Hell, though 'Me' would not admit it.

39. MASTER SNOWMAN

Sometimes, for no rational cause, I buy a copy of the *Tablet*. A recent copy contained an article condemning those who complain to Rome about the behaviour of their bishops. 'Anonymous delation is a great evil...' states the author, Clifford Longley. 'It is a charter for sneaks. It leads to a climate of resentment, division, distrust, suspicion and even paranoia.' He then goes on to write of the 'communion of mutual trust, love and respect' that should exist between a bishop and his people.

This took my breath away, for when your bishop has overseen the mutilation of your church, encouraged heresy, permitted your children to be subjected to 'modern' notions of sex education and flatly refused to answer your queries, then your instinct, your only recourse, is to apply to Head Office for clarification. Bishops, in my experience, have inflated ideas of their own importance; jacks-in-office, they succumb to the tendency of minor bureaucrats, or middle management, to throw their weight about and insist on having their own way, deaf to the anguished pleas of the parishioners. And, what's more, I have not so far found Rome sufficiently robust in dealing with them and their shenanigans.

As for the 'anonymity' of which the author writes, I wish I'd employed it when attempting to contact the late Archbishop Worlock, for the instant he knew it was I writing the letter or hanging on the end of the phone, down came the wall of silence, wallop. Our author quotes the Archbishop as moaning about a 'denunciation' of his activities and wondering who'd made it in the first place. I was once in his bad books for writing disrespectfully of one of his protégées. Did he confront me directly, fearlessly, man to man? No, he did not. He snuck behind the scenes and demanded that I be punished. This does not contribute to that much-vaunted climate of 'trust, love and respect'. I have copies of letters from parishioners (mostly pained yet polite), asking for explanation of various arresting novelties, and responses from bishops (all brief) which range from evasive to pompous to outraged, and end, 'This correspondence is now closed.'

If your priest has confided that he doesn't believe in the existence of the soul, the Virgin Birth or the Resurrection and your bishop will do nothing, then it is your bounden duty to harass the Congregation for the Doctrine of the Faith in order to ascertain the position of the Church on these matters, not merely swallow whatever fashionable tosh is being peddled in the parish.

It would be tedious to plod further through the *Tablet*, so I will mention only a piece entitled 'Question of Colour', in which 'Pastor Ignotus' twitters away about the 'exclusively white picture of God' that he fears will alienate black members of society. I don't know anyone who perceives God as a sort of master snowman, and when I read that Pastor Ignotus years ago gave up mentioning the kingdom of darkness and the kingdom of light in the Baptismal rite in case it might upset someone, and dropped, as it were, the symbolic white cloth, I found myself short of breath again. When my grandson was baptized we grabbed, at the last minute before leaving for church, a white traycloth from the sideboard, having left the usual shawl in Wales. His black father did not totter back aghast at the awful sight, nor run screaming at the mention of darkness and light. He knows, for God's sake, the difference between night and day and black things and white things and he doesn't take it personally.

40. BEGGING

I was talking to our builder the other morning as he rested a while from tearing up the floorboards. He said he'd been reading an article in a geographic magazine in which an attempt had been made to clarify, if not the meaning, then the origins of the universe. At one moment, he said the article stated, there was nothing, absolutely nothing, and then (and somewhere, in the effort to make all plain, there occurred the phrase 'to the power of 43'), in the blink of an eye, only not nearly as long as that would take, there was everything and, allowing for the passage of time, here we all are. We agreed that it was difficult to comprehend.

Then I heard a man talking about a new theory of time, a theory which holds that only the present moment exists, not the previous moment nor the next, which is incontrovertible but doesn't get us any further: a kind of ontological/pointilliste theory not unlike the idea, which affects me at times, that every moment everything is destroyed and the next is recreated. This would account for those occasions when you find yourself halfway up the stairs, wondering whether you had set out with the intention of going up or down and for what purpose. It would also go some way towards explaining the state of our streets, which brings to mind the efforts of a housewife with the attention of a goldfish, attempting to impose order on chaos, turning everything out and then forgetting to put it back, buying expensive pieces of furniture to stand on rotten floorboards, etc., seemingly inexplicable lapses in continuity which deny rational, or accepted response.

The hell with it. Charity bridges eternity and the temporal and at this moment in time (the horrid phrase seems appropriate in context), I am concerned with the meaning of this virtue. On Sundays, outside the church which I frequent, are usually to be found a few beggars, middle-aged to old men. Last week as I approached the doors I saw a well-dressed young woman clearly advising them to get lost. As I drew nearer I heard her speaking. 'Get a job,' she was saying to one elderly wreck.

'I have fits,' he responded mildly. 'Then don't have them,' said she, not at all in Christ-like tones as one who would heal, but rather as one who had found something under her shoe.

I muttered in a general sort of way that I didn't think her attitude very Christian, and she glared at me. Another woman, on her way out, implied that it was *begging* that wasn't very Christian and Father had said so and she glared at me too. Naturally, by now, I was pressing on both beggars every ounce of loose change I could dig up and they were thanking me nicely and hoping I'd have a nice day. Clearly this meant to the ladies that I was tarred with the same brush and deserving of the same treatment. They were in the grip of some powerful emotion and I will swear that it was *hate*. Very rum.

After Mass the priest said, moderately, that the beggars should not be encouraged as they spent the money on drink and used bad language. Admittedly the breath of the oldest could have taken the sheen off brass but he had not, as I might have done in his place, sworn at the young woman and I shall continue to give him my change. I've known the need of a drink myself and I'd rather give beggars money than pay £100 for some charitable ball or concert. At least I know it won't go on 'administration'.

41. *NOLI ME TANGERE*

I've seen a photograph of the statue of Christ in Trafalgar Square and I've heard a vicar uttering words to the effect that it's a very good likeness since no one knows exactly what Christ looked like and anyway He looked like everyone else – something on those lines.

My only reaction as I gazed at the photograph was that there had been one of those mistakes in identification to which witnesses are so prone: that wasn't Christ, that was just some bloke the sculptor had got to pose for him, who not only did not resemble Christ but looked very much like someone quite different. The image of Christ is protean but there are limits.

I was reminded of a truly arresting picture I once saw in an American magazine which showed Christ in collar and tie, smiling widely and looking for all the world like the Chairman of the Board of some dubious company which leaned heavily on expert PR for popular support. No one in his right senses would lay down his life for such a one as this. He might attempt to ingratiate himself with the possessor of the confident grin in the hope of furthering his own aims, but his motives would be far from pure.

People with an axe to grind are constantly seizing on the figure of Jesus and attempting to remould Him in their own image, as a gay or a freedom fighter or a female or a Bible Belt entrepreneur. One 19th-century author contrived in his *Life of Jesus* to render Him even less attractive, portraying Him, by some peculiar means, as a figure irresistibly reminiscent of Mr Gladstone. The words 'nobility' and 'sorrowful' when used too frequently have an adverse effect on the reader, conjuring up an image of an elderly, remote and disapproving personage, disappointed in his followers and beyond emulation.

Other scholars, in an attempt to apply historical and scientific values to the Gospels, have succeeded only in muddying the waters further, causing heated argument and inevitable disagreement among themselves and confusion to the faithful,

whose ranks diminish in proportion to all the supposedly help-
ful dialectic.

In an introduction to Strauss's *Life of Jesus* (1835) we read,
'Indeed if our scientists are to be believed, when they tell us that
the development of the individual is only an abbreviated repetition of the similar but much slower phases of the development
of the species, it is hardly too much to maintain, that in the
present and in the future every individual who determines to
make his way from the bondage of a naive trust in authority and
tradition into the freedom and light of mature thought must
pass through precisely that stage of thorough-going logical
negative criticism which is presented by Strauss's work in a
unique manner... The imaginary lights of mythological tradition must be put out, that the eye may distinguish the false from
the true in the twilight of the Biblical origins of our religion.'

This was written in the early days of the onset of our 'naive
trust' in scientific progress and sounds all very fine and large but
is like climbing out of the boat when the shore lies beyond the
horizon and you can't swim. Many a believer has foundered trying to penetrate the depths, let alone make landfall. We cannot
know the 'mind of God' despite certain rash claims, and since
we find it difficult to fathom our fellows and even ourselves, we
don't stand much chance of understanding Jesus in His entirety.
I don't actually believe that we're expected to. *Noli me tangere.*

42. THE DOME

The infantilism that pervades the new order of Mass becomes even more evident over Christmas, but when our Saviour said that we should become as little children I don't think he was suggesting that we should prance about as mutton dressed as lamb, or sink, mindlessly, into a second childhood. On one recent occasion I went, under protest, to a church where we were treated to a frightfully jolly sermon, rounds of applause, soppy hymns and an overall atmosphere of insufferable winsomeness. It goes without saying that there were no altar rails, communion was taken in the hand, standing and, despite the presence of two priests, offered by 'Ministers of the Eucharist', and there was a lady clutching the chalice for anyone who fancied communion under two kinds. Not many people took up the offer, but it's the thought that counts.

Afterwards I seized the opportunity to snarl at a priest. More aggrieved than astonished, he took off his smile and implied that I couldn't possibly mean I hadn't *really* enjoyed it at all; that for recondite and suspect reasons of my own I was denying what fun it had been; that I couldn't sincerely miss the old Mass which had lacked the 'spirit of community', where there hadn't been any laughs and no one had joined in singing 'Amazing Grace', which of all tunes is the one I loathe the most. Not wishing to monopolize him, I left without further explanation, but reflecting that it had come to something when I had to justify church-going to myself by remembering the martyrdoms to which better people than I had subjected themselves over the course of centuries, the joyful, spiritual satisfaction of Mass supplanted by the gloomy feeling that one was, at least, suffering a personal mortification of the senses in a good cause. A friend said consolingly that all I had to do was remember the sacrifice of the Lord which is the whole focus of the Mass, but that is quite different when the occasion is drenched in saccharine syrup and the priest is playing the homily for laughs.

And then there's the Dome. I try not to think about the

stupid thing but it does give one furiously to think when its organizers evince a stubborn reluctance to acknowledge the significance of the Millennium and insist on treating the date as an excuse 'to party', a further illustration of the hedonistic infantilism that seems to have overwhelmed not only the Church but everything else as well. As far as I can gather, the Dome is meant to house evidence of human progress over 2,000 years, which is ironic when you take a look round, and is not concerned with the life of Christ. It seems like a latter-day Golden Calf and one can only hope it falls over, since, leaving aside the Redeemer, there is very little to sing and dance about. I must confess to a certain unworthy anticipation of the chiliastic excesses which can surely be expected as yet more false messiahs make their appearance, but this is only whistling in the dark, since their comical aspects are too often superseded by their murderous inclinations and their gulled followers led to their deaths.

All in all, then, a melancholy prospect, even leaving aside the prognostications of St John the Divine. The heavenly host, the forces of darkness need hardly trouble themselves to get out of bed when the human race is proving itself so adept at self-destruction, spiritual and physical, and has learned so little from the Gospels. If anyone is planning to rebuke me for lack of faith let him have another mince pie. I do have faith, only not in our leaders, either spiritual or temporal. Happy New Year.

43. PROGRESS

'Every epoch has its own peculiar dangers and temptations. These have to be noted and avoided or conquered if that epoch is to get the full benefit of the advantages which progress has brought to it.' Thus wrote one Isabella Eyrie Mayo in 1900 in an article entitled 'The Perils of Modern Society' in *The Young Woman*, a work compiled with the manifest intention of putting females on the right lines at a time when '… we hear constantly of the mad race of wealth, of the frenzied pursuit of pleasure, of the perpetual unrest which permeate Society from the highest ranks to the lowest.' Young girls 'have lived in the utmost freedom, which they carry to the extent of cigarette smoking and betting.' If they marry they find 'the restraints of married life irksome, and it is remarkable how many women today seem to think that maternity means but the bringing forth of the babe. Mama is so seldom at home in the evening that it is no use for her to attempt to lead him through his evening prayer.' The assumption here *is* different. Vespers does not today rank high on the list of maternal commitment, while *The Young Woman* took it for granted that its readers paid at least lip service to Christianity.

Another contributor muses, 'What a long, sweet day of love's sunshine Christmas would be if every heart in this world would give out of its native abundance goodwill, cheerfulness, gentleness, courtesy, sympathy, little deeds of loving service, smiles of kindness and words of comfort.' This plea was occasioned by an episode in Edinburgh where a Christmas treat was to be given to some poor children at a mission ball. There were hundreds of them lined up and among them was a thinly clad little girl, 'alas! barefoot on the cold, hard stones.' She was hopping from foot to foot, striving in vain to keep the biting, stinging chill out of her limbs, when a boy, after watching her pityingly for a while, snatched off his cap and dropped it. 'There, lassie,' he cried, 'ye maun stand on that.' 'It was the Christian spirit', writes the author, 'welling up in that poor boy's heart that prompted the loving deed and word.'

Somewhere here there is great change. While people may retain some altruistic instincts, they are seldom expressed on the street. The State or the organized charities are expected to cope with the barefoot, and it would be a brave boy who showed simple compassion to a little girl in the presence of his mates. The 'Christian spirit' is out of fashion, though it is still fondly imagined by the optimistic that we will be kind to each other out of a feeling of common humanity. The sense of guilt, whether acknowledged or not, that gripped the Victorians with their awareness of the huge inequalities of wealth is absent, while those in power are at pains to deny that the great divide exists. It is considered commendable to accumulate vast sums of money, and eccentric, not to say reprehensible, to hand any out to people sleeping in doorways. There seems to be the feeling that the State can be trusted to minister to the unfortunate, relieving the populace of personal responsibility. The fact that this notion does not work in practice is largely unperceived.

Isabella, were she permitted to return for a look, would recognize our frantic clutching at youth and the plight of our beggars but be puzzled by our individual attitudes. Progress may have brought its advantages but few get the full benefit of them, any more than they did 100 years ago.

44. RESIGNATION

A friend folded aside her newspaper and remarked despondently that it looked to her as though the Anti-Christ had arrived unannounced and was taking over, for she had read of nothing but greed, hedonism, depravity and cruelty. Besides, what the restaurant critic and his companion had spent on lunch would have kept a family for a week, while the money required for clothes on the fashion page would have kept the same family for six months; what's more, she wouldn't have been seen dead in any of them.

At this point a proper religious writer would have assumed a wholesome expression, uttered a gentle reproof beginning, 'But ...' and gone on to itemize all the lovely things that were happening quietly among the ordinary people – only, offhand, I couldn't think of any.

All governments appear corrupt and all people indifferent except for those who have been killed, maimed, made homeless or otherwise disadvantaged. The only smiles are on the faces of the rich and powerful, the drunk and the drugged, while the rest of the populace moans discontentedly, too apathetic to rise up in revolt.

It would, admittedly, be difficult to isolate anything specific to revolt against, for the rot is insidious and ubiquitous and frequently dressed up with fancy names such as 'downsizing' or 'tolerance' or 'progress' or 'diversification', while the humanist insistence that all are basically good and well disposed to each other casts a miasma over reality. We know it's not true but it's rude to say so.

The present combination of ruthlessness and sentimentality is at least as pernicious as it was in the time of Victoria. The emphasis is different now that cant has the edge over hypocrisy, but the result is as damaging and we are bringing up our young as badly. The Victorians had optimism even if it was misplaced, and all we have is resignation: not Christian resignation but bored, resentful powerlessness.

Thinking of the young, when did the 'teenager' first strike? The Victorians didn't have any: you emerged from the nursery to take your place at the dinner table, using the correct knife and fork; or from the midden to the mill, depending on your circumstances. There was no time to indulge in interim rebellion, nor can the young, on the whole, have been as ignorant of the facts of life as we now suppose, not if they were reared in the country or lived with dozens of others of all ages in a small, confined and noisome space.

Even the privileged, unless they were remarkably dim, must have had some inkling of the actuality when babies were born and the dead laid out at home. They just didn't go on about it all the time. The newly sacrosanct belief that 'sex education' should be forced on infants is an indication not of enlightened thinking but of the distance we have travelled from what might as well be called nature.

The 'gooseberry bush', of course, had highly improper connotations, and I shall continue to tell babies that the angels brought them and in the end will take them away again. I consider there to be as much truth in this as in the purely physiological interpretation, and it's more interesting.

45. SERENITY

The quality of serenity, the opposite of despair, could, when you come to think about it, be the result of the same attitude – 'I don't give a damn' – the difference being that the serene person thinks that nothing in the world matters much, while the despairing think nothing matters at all. I once knew a man whose serenity, I suspected, arose from another source: he was pleased with himself. Many seemingly sensible people revered him for his humility and selflessness and the way he had devoted himself to good works and the assistance of the unfortunate, but something did not ring true. He had made a name for himself in the worldly sphere, had cut a dashing figure in his youth, and people gasped when he abandoned ambition to embrace poverty, but it didn't quite turn out like that. He got more famous and the wealthy poured money into his good causes. He had a roof over his head, his travelling expenses were paid, he had enough to eat and more people had heard of him than if he'd devoted his life to racing driving. They flocked to meet him and he accepted their homage with imperturbable modesty. He seldom raised his voice and his face was unlined. If things had gone differently I think he might have been diagnosed as a psychopath: I could, of course, be doing him an injustice, but he made me uneasy.

The serenity of the few holy people I have met did not rely on that curious, disconcerting appearance of passivity, nor were they given to enthusiastic displays of uncalled for affection. I recently encountered another man who hugged strangers on introduction and announced that not only he but God loved them. I was being taken round by the born-again and felt like a bad dog being taken for a walk by the curate. The direction I wished to go was not the one in which they wanted to guide me and gulfs of incomprehension opened up on every side. They reminded me of people on that much vaunted journey who have stopped off at a hamburger joint and imagine they've reached the goal.

Would that it were so simple. The path of perfection is not lined with primroses and the more you think you're on it, the likelier you are to fall off. Saints have a difficult time and can seldom relax in the accepted sense of the word: their serenity is based on a sense of eternity which puts temporal concerns into perspective but they are not in the habit of self-congratulation. Serenity based on presumption might just as well be despair for all the good it does, and the degree to which the message of Christ has been misinterpreted must cause satisfaction in Hell. The assumption that we can know Him merely by *wanting* to strikes me as over-optimistic: the disciples had trouble understanding Him and they were there. Much time and effort have been expended in the quest for the 'historical Jesus', while the God/Man is increasingly put aside as too baffling a concept to be relevant. Many of the things He said do not fit with the picture of the perfect sweetie in whose mouth butter would not melt.

The uneducated find this caricature risible and make jokes about it, which would be blasphemous if they knew what they were saying, but since they don't the poor creatures can't be held responsible.

46. UNDERSTANDING GOD

Sir Thomas Browne said, 'God has not made a single creature who can understand Him.' People keep forgetting this: they persist in defining Him, usually as someone who sympathizes with their own ideas and aspirations, or if they are too clever for that and are aware of the admittedly noticeable limitations of popular religious attitudes, they simplify matters by not attempting to see God's point of view and deny His existence. This may solve everything to their satisfaction but it makes them boring companions. Once you've covered the usual topics – the state of the crops, the sexual indiscretions of your common acquaintances, the vacuity of Mr Blair and his Cabinet, the second law of thermodynamics and the best place to buy organic bacon, etc. – a silence falls, unless, as often happens, you go through the whole rota again. How much more interesting to speculate on the nature of the Deity, inconclusive though our musings might be.

'Some one has said that the true pulpit of these latter days is the newspaper press... even poor "average humanity" cares for something beyond race-meetings, divorce cases, and scandals in high life... a new book, or a new development of thought may hope to rival even these breathless interests.' Richard Le Gallienne wrote this to his editor in 1893, going on to remark: 'We have nowadays to put up with a good deal in the way of sacrilege, but I could not stand by and see the sublime figure of Christ vulgarized to make an Adelphi holiday.' Remarkable how things don't change a lot. He wrote of the professionals of two rival doctrines, the Churchman and the Man of Science, each insisting that the subject of religious inquiry is his inviolable property; and in proof one 'brings his Bible and the other a hermetically sealed tube containing protoplasm.'

So the Man of Science now has more to show and tell than a test tube of protoplasm and the scholars are busily picking the bones out of the Bible, but we are still running on the spot in the matter of understanding God. As our author put it: 'To the one the world is opaque, shut within the walls of form and colour, to the other it is mystically transparent, palpitating with occult significance.' There are few of the 'other' at present, mystics being either in short supply or in hiding. Those who do raise a head above the parapet tend to syncretism – not wishing to offend – and rather muddy than clarify the waters, but on the whole the Christian as Social Worker is the more usual example

Le Gallienne wrote that while Christ was not so much the prophet of any absolutely new religious intuition, he gathered up into one masterful synthesis those that 'had enjoyed but an isolated expression aforetime. The intense spirituality of the Hebrew, the impassioned self-annihilation of the Hindoo, the joyous naturalism of the Greek.' This is open to the sort of argument that could enliven many an evening but may take a while to catch on again. In 1893 it seems the typical literary man of the period was sipping his absinthe with a 'charmingly boyish sense of sin' while reading Huysmans and would not have dreamt of discussing such antiquated matters as God, Love or Duty when he could be wrangling over Degas or grappling with a sonnet by Mallarmé. Substitute the artists of your choice and again – no change. Absinthe, having for a time been proscribed, is now available at certain, select venues.

47. DISTORTIONS

Lord David Cecil said Christianity has compelled the mind of man not because it is the most cheering view of man's existence but because it is truest to the facts. I think this is so, but it is increasingly being obscured by a layer of artificial sweetness to which has adhered a collection of amorphous fluff. To gentle Jesus, meek and mild have been added the liberal, the social worker and – rather less popular now but still around – the revolutionary. It must be the image of the lamb which misled the Victorians into their flowery wilderness of meekness and mildness, or perhaps a nervous, half-conscious awareness of the potentially violent nature of the young – children and colonies. It would have been in their interests to persuade the rising generation that mildness and meekness paid off in the end.

The present distortions of the Lord are also ideologically inspired, and a surprising variety of people feel free to seize the banner of Christ and plant it in the midst of their muddle of quirks and aspirations. There is too a group which calls itself Christian but holds that there is no such thing as Original Sin, seeming not to have noticed if that were so, then the presence of Christ and his Mission on Earth was an awful waste of time. Article XI of those 'wondrous little particles' got it right, stating baldly and glumly that 'man is very far gone from original righteousness and is of his own nature inclined to evil.' To many people who consider themselves Christian this would seem worse than heretical (a concept that doesn't really worry them), unnecessarily rude and even politically incorrect. These are the people who insist on employing various euphemisms for the blind, the halt, the mad: again not noticing the implications of intolerance, of patronising contempt, of the genteel fastidiousness which by declining to call a spade a spade seeks to deny its existence. By diluting the terms they veer close to denying the condition, which is in itself an expression – no matter how garlanded with roses and hung about with feathers and sweet violets – of distaste, of disapproval.

I don't think Christ would have so pussy-footed about in the presence of anguish. Jean Vanier observed: 'The danger is that we forget how to welcome and no longer see handicapped people as a gift of God'. Many of the *bien pensant* would find it hard to get their minds round that one. Faith, hope and charity have had their meanings changed: faith, to most, says 'gullible', hope is what you experience when you write out your lottery numbers, and charity is something you do when a TV personality tells you to. On another level, faith works because and in spite of the dictates of reason, depending on which direction you're looking at the time, hope is an irritation suffered by the pessimistic, for the optimist lives in expectation, and charity means selflessness. There are many ways of assessing and measuring those virtues before thoughtlessly flinging them aside as irrelevant. The accepted image of Christianity at present is one cast not so much by its enemies as by its lukewarm and ill-educated followers, rather as the accepted view of Western art is formed by contemplating structures that are merely commentaries on the state of mind of the artist.

We should wash our eyes and take another look at Jesus. T S Eliot did. In *Gerontion* he wrote: 'In the juvenescence of the year/Came Christ the tiger...'

48. SURRENDERING TO GOD

There is a common tendency to confuse spirituality with imagination, with fantasy and wish-fulfilment, but feeling cosy is not necessarily indicative of spiritual progression. There is a line in one of those superior American soaps, said of a woman who has gone to find herself. Someone remarks, 'All she had to do was look under the nearest man,' which, although rather coarse, is on the same lines as the ancient observation that you can change the skies by sailing away but not yourself. Warm feelings of contentment can be arrived at by contemplating the sunset or nestling in the long grass, drinking whisky or sniffing cocaine, but the momentary sense of being at one with the universe tends to fade, leaving you where you started, or in the latter case, several steps further back. Music, art, literature, fairy stories, all contribute to the illusion that other dimensions are readily available and infinity is there for the asking, but the quest for the mystical is like gardening in the dark – difficult and initially unrewarding.

We should regard with scepticism those who announce that they've been talking to God and have a message for us. God has never been much of a conversationalist. True mystics are few and far between and not to be envied by those who aspire to an easy life. Nor is it entirely desirable to 'find yourself'; those who are looking, in the present climate of opinion, seem to imagine that their search will be rewarded by a delightful surprise, but those who have taken an honest, clear-sighted appraisal of themselves are more frequently appalled. Learning to 'love yourself' when you really know yourself can turn out to be an impossibility. The meticulous examination of conscience is one of the trials the mystic must suffer and can be destructive if he has not already sensed the presence of the living tree in the darkness.

Nor is it allowable to be entirely passive under this weight of desolation. Some indescribable and unnamed aspect of the soul must continue to endure and to strive to be aware. A Zen master called those who closed their eyes 'the dwellers of the skeleton cave in the dark valley. Abandonment is the key to union with God for those who believe in Him, while for the Buddhist it is the 'melting...in the infinity of the *Dharmadhata*'. Either way it is not for the idle, the nervous or the hedonistically inclined. Those who have not planned on spiritual adventure but find that God has visited them unannounced and uninvited all the same are frequently ambivalent in their feelings. 'Why me?' is a not infrequent response. Surrender to God involves the suppression of the ego, a heavy requirement in the age of the individual. The vain crave only worldly recognition while the pusillanimous would prefer to slink through life unobserved, ascribing their failings to human nature and hoping (those who do not believe that the kernel dies in the shell) to be welcomed into eternity with warm understanding and minimal interrogation. But Purgatory is a place in which to squirm as though under the eye of the stern confessor or psychiatrist determined that the subjects shall know themselves.

On the other hand the Church of England has airbrushed Hell out of the picture, stating that the wicked will be consigned to a state of nothingness – which sounds not dissimilar to Nirvana. The simplest course is to be good and let who will be clever and wait for the angels to call before worrying too much.

49. MONOCHROME

Gazing out of the window at the rain last month, the words of
Swinburne came to mind:

Thou hast conquered, O pale Galilean;
the world has grown grey from Thy breath.

The 'pale' is a bit of poetic licence: anyone who spent his time
striding round the hills and deserts of Israel would have been
swarthily complexioned and necessarily of a vigorous constitution, but the suggestion that the influence of Christ washed
colour from the world is untrue and defamatory, a view perpet-
uated by those who, on the one hand, have misunderstood His
message and prefer grey – it goes with anything and minimizes
the darkness of bigotry while obscuring the uncomfortable
demands of the light – and, on the other, those who profess to a
passion for colour and the 'freedom to choose', but somehow
manage only to muddle the pigments on the palette to an
impenetrable mud in which neither colour nor form is dis-
cernible.

If the country is increasingly monochrome, the cause lies not
only in the blurring of distinction in moral terms between
black and white, but in the tendency towards homogeneity, ecumenism and the abandonment of any principle that might be
considered politically incorrect. Protestantism, the first step on
the road to either atheism or fanaticism (depending on whether
the reader has approached the Bible in a spirit of ruthless scientific enquiry or one of unquestioning credulity), began in a cold
climate, so maybe the weather is partly to blame.

Certainly the month of July in the year 2000 in the United
Kingdom did little to encourage that sense of joy which characterizes the presence of the Holy Spirit. Nor did anything else,
with the possible secular exception of the triumph of Venus and
Serena, which was uniquely satisfying.

The prospect of mass adulation as the Queen Mother reaches
her 100th year serves merely to emphasize the lack of anything
else that might occasion communal celebration, rather as the

death of Diana was the only event in the lives of many that would bring them, weeping, into the streets: evidence, not of a common, compassionate humanity but of spiritual poverty.

I suppose if England had gained some significant victory in the game of football then joy would be unconfined, but these secular celebrations frequently end in drunkenness and temporary oblivion on a wide scale, with subsequent sorrow as the hangover and the consequences make themselves apparent. The insistence of the Orangemen on expressing their glee at defeating the native Irish in the 17th century by marching round gloating is obviously ill-advised, while the Government's attempts to contribute to the gaiety of nations regularly fall flat.

When puritans of whatever type or era try to impose their will on the people, the result is some sort of backlash, and the attitude of the Government in the matter of the Dome, at once patronising and manipulative, was enough to ignite the residual spark of contrariness in the native bosom. A supposedly free people resent being told where and how to enjoy themselves.

However, it appears that Tony Blair is influenced by Hans Küng, himself a man of a grey and homogeneous turn of mind in a collar and tie, so perhaps nothing should surprise us.

50. NOT KNOWN AT THIS ADDRESS

It could be held that those who would save God's face should deny His existence. The heavenly courtiers should tell suppli- cants He is not at home, turn away all callers, pull the shutters over the windows, loose the dogs and if all else fails say: 'Not known at this address'. Who? God? Never heard of Him. A theist in protective mode might well think thus after taking a look around. He might ally himself with the atheist in order to save God from the light of publicity, the naming and shaming and the blame. Like some children of delinquent parents he might seek to distract attention from His dereliction by hiding Him away, claiming to know nothing of His intentions, past, present or future. This would be a pessimistic theist, a depressed person seeing only the darker side of human exis- tence and himself wondering why God didn't *do* something. He would see no point in being happy when, apparently, circum- stances didn't warrant it, and if he overheard someone saying, 'I never thought I'd find myself in a place like this', he would take it as a complaint, a cry of regret or even shame, when the speaker might be expressing a sense of surprised gratitude. The latter is certainly unusual, since most people are dissatisfied, but it is not impossible. Some, depending on their cast of mind, might say it in Malibu, others in the hills of Wales on a morning when it didn't happen to be raining.

What the sad theist would not do (we are assuming he has a proper sense of decorum) is ally himself with the religiously inclined who, with insensitive fervour, go round striving to impress those they meet with their own gratified awareness of being in the Lord's favour and privy to His point of view. Too often they assume that God would like to be headline news, in the public eye, and is soothed by the flashing of camera lights. False courtiers, they claim that He is always at the front door, dressed to the nines and eager for a party. They put up a lay figure, an idol, glittering, beaming and hollow, to offer a spurious welcome and encourage the crowds to draw near and prostrate themselves on the steps in a display of joy.

The sorrowful believer, if he would only apply his mind, would realize that he would be better advised to try the tradesmen's entrance and go by way of the underground rooms to look for God in the garden. He might, at first, mistake Him for the gardener, but would wait and listen for any communication that might be forthcoming. He would not, there, be disturbed by the enthusiasts clamouring in the street since they would seldom be inclined to venture through the dark rooms, filled with cobwebs and the sound of unclean creatures scattering from sight. They would not consider venturing into the garden for fear of the terrible dogs, the cold and the unstructured possibilities of things not made by man. Nor would our believer, to begin with, be entirely comfortable or at ease, but after a while he would forget what he had thought he was looking for. He had wanted God to apologize, or at least explain, but it isn't like that.

51. GROUND RULES

God speaks seldom and when He does He does so with admirable brevity and conciseness. This is one of the reasons why I like the Ten Commandments: they are blessedly free of clauses, sub-clauses, provisos, parentheses, afterthoughts and red tape. There is little scope for argument unless, of course, you disagree with the entire proposition. Thus I find no problem with the directive that we should prefer God above all things and love our neighbour as ourselves; although in the present state of unbridled consumerism, such affection should logically find expression in paying for his foreign holidays and showering him with shampoos and anti-wrinkle cream. For a moment I was dubious about my neighbour, wondering whether he could be held responsible for the proliferation of forms that we have to fill in, but I have decided that only the devil could have contrived such inhuman and largely irrelevant complexity.

The thing about the Decalogue is that it is rooted in an uncompromising acknowledgment of the limitations of human nature, and its demands are realistic. Those Utopians who believe in the perfectibility of man ask the impossible, starting as they do from the premise that we are naturally 'good' and if left to ourselves without the constraints of religion will do the right thing and be nice to each other. Then, to ensure we get the message, they interfere constantly with our lives and liberties and make us fill in forms, while the EEC with its insistence on 'rights' drives the citizen mad with baffled exasperation.

The American Constitution was in at the start of the rot. The right to the pursuit of happiness would sound stupid to anyone with an ounce of intelligence in any era, but the authors cannot really be blamed for failing to realize that the right to bear arms would lead to Americans slaughtering numbers of their neighbours in fits of pique, or that the freedom of speech might involve scenes of sadism, bestiality, paedophilia, etc., being aired in a medium yet to be conceived.

Mrs Trollope was particularly incensed with Jefferson, who was responsible for 'that phrase of mischevious sophistry "all men are born free and equal"', considering 'this great American an unprincipled tyrant and most heartless libertine', since he was the father of children by almost all his numerous gang of female slaves, and took special pleasure in being waited on by them at table. He used to say laughingly that if his children by quadroon slaves were white enough for them to pass, then 'Let the rogues go off if they can. I will not hinder them'. Mrs Trollope says disgustedly that this was received in a large party as evidence of his 'kind and noble nature'. The American taste for bad behaviour and hypocrisy in their leaders seems to have started early.

God is too downy an old bird to go into small print. He laid down the ground rules and left us to get on with it. Some people complain about this and wish He would sometimes take a hand in affairs, but imagine how they would feel if He did, and sent us forms to fill in to gauge our reaction.

52. UNFASHIONABLE

I know a man who went to California and became a living god. Previously he had travelled widely in search of himself and had consulted various gurus. One of them, by whom he was much impressed, was herself a living god but she disapproved of homosexuality so he had, regretfully, to withdraw from her orbit, but seeing that she was on to a good thing he decided to do likewise and, rather than follow in her footsteps, make footprints of his own. Now, having reached the peak of gurudom, he has made a lot of money and gained many followers, while his writings are widely read by the sort of people who do widely read in the genre. My late husband dismissed him as a silly little twerp and went on to think about something else, but I brood on the phenomenon.

The one of whom I speak is the only one I have known at all well, but I have occasionally brushed against others and have been unable to discern whatever it is that causes the more susceptible to creep to their feet and gaze up at them. Their devotees will tell you that you cannot fail to be aware of the power of their personalities and the radiance that emanates from them, but you can. I was once taken by a friend to meet a guru she had dug up somewhere and he was at least as shifty a character as my acquaintance the living god, even if his claims were slightly more modest and he was merely 'enlightened' rather than deified. We had to sit on the floor while he uttered, at best, a few platitudes and exuded his aura. I got cramp and swiftly grew to hate him.

It has been suggested to me that since I am so unreceptive in these matters, I might have been one of those who fidgeted during the Sermon on the Mount, but I don't think so. I know sense when I hear it and can differentiate between that and the sound of the tap running. The truly worrying thing about charlatans such as the above is that people swallow their gibberish and look no further, just as people satiate themselves on junk food and never take proper nourishment. Insistence on self is the hallmark of false doctrine: self-realization; self-gratification; what used to be known as simply selfishness. Peace of mind is doubtless desirable but solipsism is a weird way of going about it and no comfort on the deathbed. Christ is an unfashionable figure, epitomising as He does self-sacrifice, and there are those who grow uneasy at Easter, wanting to have a good time and be joyful about something, but feeling that the occasion is marred by the spectacle of a tortured man and the suggestion that we too should seek to emulate him, even accepting pain and death rather than making whoopee.

Besides, Christ is politically incorrect, being against sin and insufficiently inclusive. The wetter Christians fail to mention they edit out His more uncomfortable pronouncements and seek to make Him more palatable to our self-indulgent and permissive society. I cannot forget the one who rewrote the Paternoster in his own words, improving on it and bringing it up to date: 'Our Father and Mother in whom is heaven...' Oh God.

53. BECAUSE I'M WORTH IT

The Archbishop of Canterbury says we have become a nation of atheists. Another clergyman has privately said that in his opinion the Anti-Christ is already among us. You have to be able to picture Christ in order to conceive of the opposite, and as the usual image of Him is now the popular distortion which would render Him unrecognisable to His Mother, this presents difficulties. The Archbishop takes the accepted view that religion, in order to regain its appeal, must alter to suit contemporary circumstances and, by extension, mores, but that means crawling further out along the branch to the frail and wavy end. Unless you remember the roots you end up (to put it another way) with the game of Chinese Whispers where the final message bears no reference to the original statement and you might as well forget the whole thing, which is what Dr Carey fears is happening.

He says that we, instead of addressing ourselves to the advisability of preparing for the afterlife, are more concerned with extending this one and turn to science as the source of hope, seeking avidly for temporal happiness and the alleviation of pain. This is ironic considering that science and the advance of technology have gone a long way towards disrupting the viability of the entire planet and throwing the future of the race in doubt, but mankind is notoriously short-sighted, and despite the best efforts of the clergy we have no prophets or seers, only spin-doctors and, to quote Alan Bennett, who was speaking in another context, people who make a beeline for the wrong end of the stick.

People like Lavinia Byrne who, finding the rules not to their taste, leave the organization complaining that the requirement to stick to the rules is 'bullying'. She wrote, as you may have heard, a book about women 'priests' which did not find favour with the Vatican: a consequence which seems greatly to have astonished her, making one wonder where she's been. The resistance to women 'priests' has nothing to do with 'equality', but springs from the doctrine that the priest saying Mass stands *in persona Christi*. The current fad for gender-bending is not relevant here.

Now Lavinia Byrne has written another book, *The Journey is My Home* (Hodder, £14.99), not remarkable for its impartiality in regard to herself and containing lines like: 'Reverend Mother has since told me that the image was unforgettable: the little girl [Lavinia] with the clouds of curly hair who was half in and half outside the room [symbolic], kicking her heels on the paint-work [little rascal] in order to twist around and gaze at the view[sweet]. The book has big pictures of Lavinia inside – Lavinia plays in a paddling pool, Lavinia stands by her cow, Lavinia goes to China, Lavinia is awarded an honorary degree, etc. etc.... I suppose it must be that feminism has no time for humility: the words *Domine non sum dignus* from the altar rail are drowned out by the squawk from the cosmetic counter: 'Because I'm worth it.'

54. MISS MANNERS SAYS

Here's one for Miss Manners. Reading of the Hindu festival of Khumb Mela, I was reminded of an occasion some years since when I thought, in my innocence, that it would be nice, since they were both in town, to ask two of my Indian friends to dinner. Actually one, who shall be known as A, was a friend of my late husband and the other, B, a friend of my daughter, so there was some disparity in age, but I didn't think that would matter. I have found that due to the general decline in standards there is now little difference between the attitudes of the old and young.

What I had failed to take into account, even as I remembered to keep the whole thing vegetarian out of courtesy to A, was the Hindu caste system. A was a Rajput and B a member of the merchant class and there was a frostiness around the table that I could not dispel. A, addressing himself specifically to me, told a story of how he had once been on a train and found himself, to his dismay, sitting opposite a well-dressed man who, his instinct had told him, was undoubtedly an Untouchable. I was quite lost as to what my response should be. I was certainly not about to express disapproval of A's views, but neither could I summon any warm sympathy for his plight. It got worse, for he went on to describe how, on leaving the train and going up the escalator, he had passed a young woman who had resembled both his lovely niece and my lovely daughter and she had been in the company of a black man. I was clearly expected to exhibit symptoms of horror, but all I could do was pray that my daughter and my black son-in-law, who were out for the evening, would forget my pleas that they should return early in order to chat to B over the coffee and biscuits.

This was not due to cowardice, for I have often entertained Christians, Jews and Muslims at the same time and dealt, or not, with any differences of opinion that might have arisen, and I have been known to be rude to atheists, Protestants and New Age Catholics even as they ate my salt, but this was more complex. There seemed nowhere to begin. A's prejudices were far older and stranger than our tolerances, and besides I was fond of him. It was odd to think that in some matters we had no common ground at all.

I don't know what Miss Manners or one of our all-inclusive ecumenists would suggest, but I have concluded that in future I must be more careful about guest lists and *placement* and not fling persons of conflicting beliefs together. It is not up to me to lecture anyone or to manifest disapproval of their ancient habits, no matter how regrettable I may find them. It spoils the fun if some people sit around sulking, while those who imagine themselves as able to bring about reconciliation between peoples of opposing values are invariably in for a rude shock. We are not about to see peace on earth, and until the lion and the lamb can sit comfortably together then as far as I'm concerned they must eat separately. Lions and lambs both have their points, but as long as they don't agree I'm not going to interfere.

55. MAGIC AND SCIENCE

Some years ago I was discussing with one of our finest minds the status and relationship of religion, magic and science. He held that religion and magic were the same thing and I said not so: it was magic and science that matched. Religion, properly conducted, was primarily concerned with the worship of God and went no further than asking Him to intervene and alter the state of affairs when they were inconducive to human contentment, individual or general, while magic attempted to directly interfere in and change the course of nature. Miracles were made by God and were unusual, and spells were cast by human beings and didn't work.

I could see why a trained intellect would find all this unsatisfactory and seek for something at once more utilitarian and more intellectually responsible, but the alchemist's quest for the philosopher's stone and the scientist's hunt for some gene of longevity, or indeed immortality (did they once think they'd found it in the fruit fly or did I dream that?), are similar in kind.

The scientist's white coat may not be adorned with moon and stars but his goal is the same as that of the wizard – power; while the large commercial operations would find a means of justifying the turning of their grandmothers into gold (it would lead to a cancer cure, alleviate the conditions in the Third World, add credence to the euro, etc., etc.) if they could only discover the method. Conversely, the purest religious inclination is to do God's will and not to disorder His arrangements.

This can, of course, be taken too far: it is hard to see the point, temporal or eternal, of sitting for years in one position under a tree or up a pole. Such a course adds little to the sum of human happiness, and while it must be admitted that God is unknowable it is difficult for most of us to understand why anyone should imagine He would find the spectacle gratifying.

The attempt to master all human desire can lead the practitioner to eccentric lengths, though he is seldom as dangerous as the person who wishes to exercise ultimate control over his environment. The man I was talking to believed that science would eventually solve all human problems and lead to some sort of earthly Utopia, so when I say he was one of our finest minds I mean it in the sense that he was good at figures and discerning patterns under the microscope. He was of limited use in, say, the supermarket, the wider world where the religious, provided they are free of fanaticism, move with comparative ease, accepting its limitations and trying, in their modest way, to ease its discomforts.

The second law of thermodynamics appears to be out of style. Very few scientists now find it politic to remind us that the more we meddle the more we hasten the end, when all will return to dust.

Some religious people, on the other hand, can hardly wait, and I don't know which is the more worrying.

56. THE SHOCK OF RESURRECTION

I had not been long in the deceptive calm of rural Wales when someone remarked wistfully, 'An awful lot of people die,' which is of course an understatement; but in the past few weeks within a small radius, apart from natural deaths, two young men have been killed in a car crash and yet another farmer has hanged himself; while in London, just around the corner from our old house, somebody has been cutting up young women and putting them in the canal.

I have never worked out a suitable form of words for use in the presence of death, either to the bereaved or, since I am of an anthropomorphic turn of mind, to the Grim Reaper himself. I can only think of 'Go away' or 'Welcome', depending on the circumstances.

And when he has borne off his latest victim – or charge, again depending on how you look at it – then for a while silence seems the only appropriate medium for the continued existence of the living: the babble of counselling and consolation often only prolongs and distorts what is presently horridly known as 'the grieving process.'

But mourners, even if not of previously good character, are expected to behave with courtesy and circumspection when matters turn tragic and are not supposed to tell the comforters – even the transparently insincere – to shut up. Death offers the worst nuisances the chance to express themselves without meeting the usual protests from those around them, while the bereaved have to suffer their ministrations and appear grateful. A sore trial on top of everything else.

Another annoyance regularly crops up in American films when someone has passed away – usually Mommy (though as Noel Coward once put it, 'She didn't pass on, pass over or pass out, she *died*') – someone else, usually Mommy's best friend, though sometimes her 'partner', will explain to the bereft child who wishes to know where his mother is now, that she is being kept alive in the loving hearts of the living and that this constitutes heaven.

This dismally unsatisfactory theory can console no one and has no basis in theology, mythology or even common sense. Anyone, of any age, with a grain of intelligence will see at once that being remembered is of no practical use to the deceased if she is, to all intents and purposes, body and soul, as dead as a door nail for ever and ever.

There are those who claim not to mind this lowering prospect, but for those who prefer to look on the bright side, Easter is the time. With the belief in a future event – the startling shock of resurrection – there is no need to consign the dead to the short and moth-balled shelf life of memory where only the past has (brief) significance.

As St Paul said, more or less, if Christ be not risen, then there isn't much point in anything, and you might just as well forget it. But Christ is risen, He is risen indeed.

57. SEX

⁓ ⚓ ⁓

There is a tendency among a certain type of cleric to dribble over the ideal of sexuality. Not just in the usual way which is currently indicated by the utterance 'Phwooar', but in a high-minded, an intellectual and what they would like to be understood as a spiritual way. They are no longer concernced with the love of God, which they consider not only a bit too arcane to be appreciated by the masses but also old hat and, in some subtle way, at once exclusive and divisive – two of the naughtiest words in the religious lexicon – so they don't bother with Him. What they put all the emphasis on is 'love of neighbour'. They put far more weight on this concept than it is capable of sustaining and, maybe because they see it crumbling away before their eyes, they refine it down to the love between spouses – or, of course, partners. The command to love is most vividly expressed in sexuality within marriage, they say winsomely, not neglecting to hint, for those who might feel excluded or hurt (another favourite word in the religious lexicon) that sometimes it might be all right to enjoy a spot of fornication without going to all the trouble of actually getting married, because, after all, Love is the Thing. All of which is patently nuts and worthy of D. H. Lawrence or Barbara Cartland, who despite a certain difference in style, shared a similar approach to the relations between men and women.

In passing, does anyone think of a spouse as a neighbour? To most minds, a neighbour is a person who lives not with you but next door, owns that loathsome ginger tom but is owed a certain degree of civility in the interests of keeping the peace. Loving him is a matter of consideration, kindness and the careful avoidance of meddling in his private affairs, while marriage often offers a person the opportunity to exercise control with the minimum of courtesy. In most grown-up circles the fairytale myth of happy-ever-after is discarded – nowadays probably from about the age of two and a half – as what men call 'reality' impinges ever earlier on human consciousness. Those damp-eyed clerics with the scent of orange-blossom in their nostrils seem unaware of the extent of domestic violence, the escalating divorce rate or the long-recognized fact that the first fine flush of romantic love lasts, on average, about six months.

Whereupon the love affair is either abandoned or turns into something less thrilling but with a sightly better chance of enduring for at least a while, as long as the contestants – sorry, partners – are capable of considering someone other than themselves for five minutes at a time. Arranged marriages sometimes work quite well, but the clerics of whom I speak would not approve of that. Sexual passion is the new religion and marriage the fig-leafed concession to the ragged remains of orthodoxy. One cleric has pondered the possibility that resurrection might be experienced as a great big orgasm. They all appear to keep their souls in the same drawer as their underpants.

58. THEME PARK OF
THE SPIRIT

The Archbishop of Canterbury recently revealed that he has become interested in New Age thought. He said has been reading the works of Matthew Fox. Matthew Fox is an ex-Dominican who runs – if I remember correctly – something called the Institute of Creation Spirituality (something like that) in California and employs as his second-in-command a witch who styles herself Starhawk. He follows the teaching of Teilhard de Chardin, who had, so it is alleged, a hand in the Piltdown Man scam. The movement is characterized by woolly and wishful thinking and takes no heed of the Second Law of Thermodynamics, or, as far as I can judge, the tenets of Christianity.

Another witch, native to these isles, has expressed a desire to see paganism included in the school curriculum, and, all in all, the last 2,000 years of Christian belief begin to look like a bit of a waste of time. Christ is mocked on the radio and TV and in the newspapers. For example: 'To make matters worse she can't even choose the baby's name herself and learns that the baby's name will be an expletive. I suppose Jesus Christ is better than Jesus Wept or Christ Onabike'. This bit of cheap nastiness is not untypical of the venom hardly concealed by what its per-petrators must consider to be humour, which is now rife: an adolescent trait indicative of warped development and pitiful ignorance. Meanwhile people such as Druids, who have not the remotest idea of what their erstwhile namesakes got up to, demand respect. Others flock to soothsayers and crystal-gazers or go off to commune with the fairies.

There is a developing theme park of the spirit, where the ersatz is preferred to the real, and just as junk food takes the place of true nourishment so does burgeoning twaddle and the demand for instant gratification take the place of faith and endurance, God knows whatever happened to intelligence, let alone the quest for holiness. Maybe we have not even a theme park but a sort of landfill site where rubbish piles on rubbish, our politicians are less than admirable and our entertainers dross, while our religious leaders, not wishing to appear judgemental, smirk nervously on the sidelines or, worse, seek to join in the fun. I have just heard of a vicar who has rewritten the New Testament in limerick form: 'There was a young chappie called Jesus, Whose purpose on earth was to please us' – which is not sound theology, apart from anything else.

The blasphemers, consumed by the common human urge to defile, confine themselves to mocking Christianity, whose followers no longer burn heretics or even subject them to a cross word. This is entirely in keeping with the teachings of Jesus, whose message was one of forgiveness, but it would be interesting to see the reactions of the adherents of other religions if they were given the comic treatment. We can be sure that if such a thing came to pass our bishops would be among the first to protest. They just seem to think it not quite proper to defend their own, preferring on the whole to apologize.

59. LOAVES AND FISHES

My daughter told me the other day of an incident that happened during a stroll she was taking with her son, aged three, in Toronto. She had let him run ahead in a traffic-free area when she saw, as she put it, the dirtiest, smelliest, foulest old tramp in the whole of Ontario offering Isaac half his sandwich. Isaac, gratified and appreciative of this unexpected treat, had opened his mouth to receive it when his mother, screeching, leapt forward and scooped him up. I hoped, I said, that she explained that the child was allergic to nuts and intolerant to egg, and she said she would have done if she had thought of it in time. I brooded over the implications of the scene: the charming kindliness of the tramp's gesture, the spontaneity of the child's acceptance and the miserable circumstances that led necessarily to rejection and the breakdown of relations between two human beings. In the end I blamed the progress of science, which has come to the point where the excessive attention to hygiene and its over-effective products means that the human frame can no longer cope with germs it would have once shrugged off.

What would happen now in our affluent society if a few thousand people were gathered together to listen to an orator and found that baskets of loaves and fishes were being passed round? Even those who would cheerfully buy dubious hot dogs and hamburgers from itinerant vendors would probably refuse free food, asking themselves what the game was, while the prudent would decline the offerings on the grounds that the fish might be farmed and full of dioxins and the bread not innocent of gluten and possibly contaminated by peanuts, and anyway, how could they be sure it had been prepared under controlled conditions by supervised handlers with their hair out of the way under a hat?

The modernist reading of the miracle of the loaves and fishes is that the people, moved to altruism by the words of Our Lord, had, all at once, handed out the constituents of their picnics to their neighbours. But I find this unlikely. Not so much that I doubt their willingness to share, I just believe that many of them would not have had the forethought to pack a snack before hastening out. It seems ever more improbable the more I try to picture the scene. Admittedly, my imaginings are themselves contaminated by unbidden, incongruous images of biblical robes falling apart to reveal neatly packaged victuals in Tupperware boxes or even wrapped in ancient copies of the *Jerusalem Post*, but that's all by the by.

What is really interesting is not only the vexed question of whether we should give to beggars, but whether we should receive from them. No one who was not a child or a saint or out of his mind would eat half a sandwich which had probably been discarded by a third party in the nearest rubbish bin, but since the sharing of food is one of the oldest courtesies in the world (the literal meaning of the word 'companion' is 'one with whom you share bread') and goes a long way towards defining our humanity, our present fastidiousness, no matter how well-founded, serves to illustrate what a mess we have brought ourselves to.

60. AN INCLUSIVE CHURCH

Listening to yet another bishop talking, I wondered how Christianity in this country had got to its present state. Although I did not live through the muscular phase, I was aware of its influence, associating it with long walks, cold baths and manly chats round the camp fire. Now the Church of England seems to be dominated by middle-aged ladies with short grey hair and formidable fronts.

Actually they turn up in the Catholic Church too, exuding their own brand of pious fatuity in the guise of common sense, and are bossier than the old-style parish priest, though less concerned with sin and more with political correctness.

Some of them believe in fairies as well as angels and think the sceptic wickedly unkind, for heresy is of little significance as long as we all believe in whatever it is the other person is currently believing in and are under no circumstances 'judgemental'.

The Catholic Church has slithered all over the place, alienating vast numbers of its followers in its anxiety not to appear old-fashioned, and the result is grey and lumpy and fluffy and soggy, like a badly ordered wash in too much dirty water. The Church wants to be inclusive and relevant and sweet, so treats its members as though they were incapable of coping with reality. The tone of the homily is often that of the kindly nursery nurse in charge of a number of naughty but lovable children who must be indulged and never subjected to rebuke.

I was going to say that this was an increasing tendency but I think, please God, that it has gone about as far as it can go. It is disconcerting to be met, American-style, at the church door by a lay person. It reminds me of those maddening messages in large stores that say, 'Thank you for shopping with us.' One does not go there to gratify the company or the personnel, one goes for one's own purposes.

Nor does one need to be coaxed into church and made a fuss of. I prefer the company of my fellow man if I meet him not in a church but in a bar; the atmosphere of bonhomie is more plausible. There used to be something satisfying and not incongruous about going to Mass, which was once unapologetically concerned with God, and thence to the pub over the road, where I would find myself warmly inclined to the aforesaid fellow man, since no one had been insisting that I shake him by the hand.

If they persist in treating us like children, they should at least be aware of the usual childish response to platitudinous and patronising directives. On being exhorted to behave as you would otherwise be naturally inclined to, it is common to mutter, 'Shan't.'

Human nature is undoubtedly flawed, but the present all-pervasive approach towards remedy is well off course. Bishops and politicians – with sadly few exceptions – are infuriating.

61. WORSHIPPING WOMEN

Adherents of the new Christian movement continue in their enthusiastic efforts to make a dog's breakfast of the whole thing. A lady priest, seemingly unfamiliar with, or dismissive of, the tale of Job who 'sinned not nor charged God foolishly', announces that she sometimes calls God a bastard: laughter. She has an affliction and is understandably upset, but hastens to add that she is more concerned about the afflictions of others. ''Course you are, darling', as our friend the used-car salesman would say.

The 'brute and blackguard' cry properly belongs to adolescence, but some feminists have hauled it up in apparent justification of their grievance. They whinge tirelessly about the misogyny of the Catholic Church, but when it comes to loathing the opposite sex, they are peerless. It might seem odd that their rage should be directed at an institution that has frequently been accused (wrongly, but as they don't seem to know much about theology or tradition, they probably don't know that either) of worshipping a woman, but they are uneasy about the Virgin Mary. She is insufficiently 'feisty' for their tastes – all that handmaiden of the Lord stuff and 'be it unto me according to Thy word', and she never really came out as a founder member of the sisterhood. She is best not mentioned. Besides, the feminists sometimes like to call God 'her' as a sort of compliment since they so despise the male, and since Our Lady is the mother of Christ, the imagination begins to boggle at the question of parenthood. It is annoying for them that Christ Himself appeared to be in no confusion about the matter, being quite clear about who His mother was and addressing God as Father. And then, with a startling lack of taste, forethought or consideration, He chose men as His disciples.

The feminists should really concede that the Judaeo-Christian tradition is not for them and go off and dance in circles somewhere else. But it may well be that they wish to destroy the Church from within, in that maggoty, Marxist fashion, and are determined to re-form Christ as the androgynous fruit of a lesbian union. Such flights of fancy are also termed by their perpetrators 'development of doctrine.'

Another group gathered recently in order to demand that ladies should be allowed to be priests (rather as MPs fuss about foxes while the world around shows signs of disintegrating), and is further evidence of a peculiar sense of priorities. With the troubles present and looming that we have to overcome, the insistence on the pre-eminent importance of sexual homogeneity seems misplaced, not to say mad. I believe that if forced to choose with whom I would prefer to spend a few hours, I would opt for football hooligans rather than face the malignant ferocity of a roomful of would-be lady priests and discontented nuns. It was a woman, after all, who advised: 'Curse God and die.'

62. FORGIVENESS

I could be wrong, but I think Christianity is the only religion to preach forgiveness as one of its chief tenets, with particular emphasis on forgiving your enemies. It is, in fact, often rather harder to forgive your nearest and dearest when they step out of line. Your enemy might well be a complete fathead and a moral idiot, but you feel your loved ones should know better. The cry 'How *could* you be so naughty/stupid' is frequently heard at family gatherings.

I don't really know what forgiveness is or what form it should take: when you have yourself 'hurt the one you love, the one you shouldn't hurt at all', as the song has it, your first wish is not to be forgiven but to undo the harm you have inflicted and make the injured party happy again. Apologies are in order but frequently seem inadequate and the ensuing remorse can be out of proportion to the damage. Worse offenders, thieves and murderers, often feel no remorse at all, and there is no point in forgiving them since they would fail to appreciate such magnanimity. It could be argued that the refusal to bear animosity lightens the spirit, but the unfortunate truth is that nothing lifts the heart as much as the knowledge that the offender has got his just deserts.

This is where we rely on the law, which so often lets us down, indulging malefactors and appearing as the instrument of anarchy rather than of justice: there have been several recent examples of egregious injustice masquerading under a cloak of legality, causing outraged incomprehension in the public and leading to the urge to resort to private vengeance. This is how vendettas begin, and once begun they go on for generations, since few people have the moral authority or courage to put a stop to the bloody business by making a conscious act and declaration of forgiveness. Such an act could be perceived as weakness or cowardice and anyway, forgiveness does not bring the same horrid satisfaction as an act of vengeance: if the populace is to mend its manners, then the State (or whatever) must keep order.

I once identified what I called the Lord Longford Syndrome (God rest his soul), which consists in forgiving someone for something he has done to someone other than yourself. People get very annoyed at this attitude. It is hard enough, when you are bleeding, to be told to forgive the aggressor, but intolerable to see somebody else going ahead and forgiving him/her without so much as a by-your-leave.

Christianity, when viewed from some angles, is a very odd religion, seeming to make fewer concessions to human nature than any other, and it is remarkable that it has survived as long as it has. The difficulty lies not so much in its seeming irrationality as in its pragmatism, for clearly if forgiveness was more widespread there would be far less trouble in the world, but the human race is not prepared to try it. Vengeance is mine, saith the Lord, but I begin to think forgiveness is His too, and only His. We don't know quite how to do it.

63. A CASE OF ATTEMPTED SUICIDE

The Church of England has long been recognized as a forcing ground for chumps, but the tendency has spread further. The Archbishop of Westminster says on a note of regretful, though mild, surprise that Christianity is nearly vanquished in Britain. It does not seem to have occurred to him that 'vanquished' is not the *mot juste*, but that the Church is rather a case of attempted suicide, its garments – tradition, authority, faith, beauty, liturgy – littering the shoreline. Or, if that appears too extreme, then it could be seen as the victim of several modern neuroses: the urge to look good in a casual, undemanding way, even in the eyes of the enemy; the craven desire not to give offence, even to the enemy; and, in a final contortion, hell-bent on administering to itself the *coup de grâce* by identifying with the enemy, which for purposes of brevity may here be defined as liberalism.

The Church has more or less sacrificed its unique and recognisable form and lost sight of its purpose, and all – the perpetrators would claim – from the highest human motives. Chumps, most of them, but others may be convicted of malice. Not, of course, the Archbishop of Westminster, or of Canterbury, who is in agreement with his fellow cleric, but those with ideas of their own who would like to force all society to contribute to their cause and who bleat endlessly about inclusivity, which too often translates as entryism. Having endeavoured to strip the Faith of its distinguishing characteristics, the bishops give vent to bewildered lamentations and wonder what has happened and why, never, naturally, investigating their own actions. Canterbury, baffled, turns to a layman to head a review of his role, and Westminster says he thinks the future of Christianity lies in new movements 'such as Youth 2000 and New Faith, and in small bible-study and prayer groups.' This is the thinking of the purveyor of snake oil, albeit one who truly believes in his potions. Since a small dose has not brought about the desired result, he empties the bottle down the throat of the patient, and no one is more amazed and unhappy than he when the patient expires.

The strength of the Faith lay in its integrity. Fragmented into these little groups, bible studying and praying all by themselves, it has gone the way of Protestantism; the old heresies poke up their heads and start again arguing with each other. Unrestrained by the confines of priesthood, the way is clear for charlatans, egoists and all manner of inadequates vying for leadership; personality cults burgeon, individuals swell out of their boots, the dopy, who are legion, fall in behind them, and ignorance and idiocy prevail. When anything goes, sooner or later the Archbishops will open their eyes and enquire in pained astonishment where everything went. The liberal trust in the basic sense of the human being is misplaced. Just look around.

64. PEOPLE OF THE BOOK

One of the more amusing aspects of the Salman Rushdie affair was the stunned astonishment of the English literary establishment when faced with the proposition that to some people something was of more importance than free speech. It doesn't seem so funny now. Total mutual incomprehension, when it doesn't end in shared indifference, usually leads to trouble. Old Welsh people finding themselves in this situation would shake their heads gloomily and say that since one was in the potato field and the other in the turnip field there was little prospect of communication and no hope of a happy outcome, and when it comes to gulfs there is none greater than that between those who believe in God and those who don't. It is wider and more difficult to bridge than the gulf between different religions. Those who hold that the definition of a religious maniac is someone who believes in God will never see the other point of view, let alone take it seriously, and people whose beliefs are not taken seriously often go mad with rage. It is inconceivable to the secular-minded that anyone would choose to go to a place of worship on the designated day rather than the seaside or supermarket, let alone welcome death in the name of the cause.

I have had discussions with Muslims and remained on amicable terms, although, once, on the way to Port Said, I was bored by the dissertation on what he insisted on calling 'Crucifiction' (methodically spelled) by the driver who was my host at the time. Did I really imagine, he demanded, that God would allow His messenger to die in that undignified fashion? There was not the remotest point in arguing. Subsequently I avoided him, and spent the time with his wife, with whom I had most things in common. She knew folk tales which don't appear in the *Arabian Nights* and we had identical opinions on the question of waste. Sitting by the sea, having finished a takeaway meal of barbecued chicken and corn cobs, she carefully gathered the bits of paper to dispose of later and scattered the remains among the stones, saying that even if the feral cats rejected them, they might appeal to the snakes.

I also admired the way in which she quietly but firmly controlled the family. We had similar opinions of menfolk, but she exhibited a remarkable degree of strategic skill in guiding matters in the direction she preferred. She gave the impression of being sustained by religion to an extent where she felt no need to scream about either it or her circumstances, and she avoided argument with serene assurance. The Western passion for dialogue leads only to trouble, whether between couples or nations: when people go to the trouble of spelling out their views the result is usually a common realization that they have even less in common than they first thought. I have never felt the need to argue with the 'People of the Book', but atheists annoy me. I remember some evenings round the dining-room table...

65. A CHILD'S VISION OF GOD

The other day, on the way back from his nursery school, my daughter's child, having eaten a sandwich, was starting on the plastic wrapper which had enveloped it when his mother told him not to. 'Why?' enquired the child. 'Because you'll die,' responded his exasperated parent, negotiating her way round a creaking tractor. 'I want to die,' confided the child after a moment's reflection. 'I want to go and see God. Don't you want to go and see God, grandmother?' These were his exact words, which I have translated into comprehensible English since I recently had to hack through some of Sir Walter Scott's Scots and have vowed never again to attempt to convey any peculiarities of accent or pronunciation in writing.

Having been directly addressed, I felt unable to answer in the usual adult fashion ('Don't be silly, dear,' 'Ask your father,' etc.) and found myself at a loss. I could not say that there was nothing in the world to measure up to trying to see God as that might have been construed as encouragement to eat clingfilm, and I could not say 'No' since that could be nothing but deleterious to the child's faith in me, if no one else. Simple questions being the hardest to answer, I took the politician's way out and talked about something else. I could have said that it was a consummation devoutly to be wished, only it was not for us to choose the means or the moment, but he would instantly have asked 'Why?' again, as children will, and it is confusing enough discussing theology with adults, let alone infants, who have the same tendency to stick to the point that distinguishes the fanatic, leaving little room for shades of opinion.

It was easier for the Victorians to talk about death since they had, perforce, to think about it all the time as their children succumbed to numberless ailments, one after the other, and they could be what we call 'sentimental' about it without arousing contempt. If we are to believe the writers of the time, the outward expression of emotion was not only tolerated but expected and our ancestors, contrary to the received wisdom, would probably consider us sadly repressed.

I don't know what the child was hoping for in his vision of God and I don't really know where he got the idea, for no one in his immediate circle is much given to pious utterances. Maybe it's one of those old-fashioned 'clouds of glory' things and he is still trailing a stray waft.

I don't think, psychology notwithstanding, that any adult can understand the child's mind.

66. TELEVISION

I thought I'd watch some television over the Christmas period as a relaxation. I leave it turned on every evening, but I don't actually watch it in the accepted meaning of the word; I just like to see it flickering in the corner beside the log fire, chattering away to itself while I 'work'. It does comedy series too, but most modern entertainment is hopelessly boring if it does not involve crime (good *v* evil), and vulgarity is no substitute. It is preferable to find one's attention momentarily caught by an uncontrolled motor vehicle than by a poor actor making some scatological utterance in a desperate grasp at humour.

At one point, I saw an early version of *The Secret Garden*, which was interesting since it was much darker (not just because it was mostly shot in black-and-white) than the later diluted and sweetened offering in which mere misunderstanding was held to blame for the children's plight. Then I wanted to watch *The Wicker Man*, but it was on so late that I fell asleep during the hymn to the landlord's daughter and saw no more. The bit with the maypole reminded me of the Thirties ('Round the maypole frolics Miss Prism, clearly not knowing its symbolism'), when the newfound enthusiasm for paganism was regarded by the sceptical with mild amusement, before it became apparent that Hitler was impressed by Madame Blavatsky, and all that Norse gods and race stuff was festering in Nazi circles. It is odd that confirmed atheists now seem to consider paganism less deleterious to human happiness – and progress and maturity and wisdom and whatever else it is they think the human race capable of – than any of the major religions, although Christianity is the only one they feel free to hold in overt, blatant contempt.

Watching the documentary channel I learned that the more refined Romans were shocked by the treatment meted out to Boudicca and her daughters by the low-class Romans, and even more appalled when the Iceni, in turn, rudely murdered upper-class Roman ladies: it was not so much the cruelty as the disrespect. In a programme about the witches of Salem someone said that the people of the time could never be certain whether they were predestined for salvation or damnation, no matter how they comported themselves, and that this caused confusion. One can see it would not have been conducive to a clear-sighted approach or a proper examination of conscience: a helpless gamble, a sort of plaything-of-fate situation – just like paganism.

I prefer (although it is not altogether a matter of choice but of conviction, since I am not one of those who, seeing the words *Mene mene tekel upharsin* appearing on the walls of the dining room, would go on buttering a roll) to believe in a just and, on the whole, forgiving deity. It is better to have a contract than a lottery ticket.

67. REMORSE

⟨꙰⟩⟨ꙮ⟩

The word 'remorse' is infrequently heard: sometimes a judge will say disapprovingly of a cold-eyed felon that he had shown none, and will sentence him more harshly than he would otherwise have done. But if the aforesaid felon has been through our present educational system he has most probably never encountered the concept, let alone heard the word. Schools seem to consider it a primary duty to foster in their pupils a sense of self-esteem, and teachers are warned never to shout at them or call them names, and, while the young are instructed not to hurl racist or sexist insults, no one seems to care much if they call a teacher a silly old git (to put it mildly), self-expression being considered so valuable in the formulation of the young mind.

It must be difficult for a person reared in an atmosphere in which a sense of guilt is considered an affliction, a worrying medical condition, to overlook the influences of a lifetime and accept personal blame. It would feel all wrong, out of step with the *zeitgeist*, oddly disrespectful, and would put the malefactor at odds with his counsellor. Nobody is supposed to have a sense of sin, a superstitious relic from an earlier, less enlightened age, and aberrant behaviour is considered to be due to, if not a chemical imbalance, then childhood deprivation.

It all goes back to the notion that mankind is basically good and that, under the right circumstances, people will be nice to each other in a natural sort of way, although seeing that the circumstances we live under are the only ones we've got and all the recent movements to radically alter them have only made them worse, this seems unrealistic.

The seriously bad are called psychopathic, incapable of empathy, not the sort to say 'I feel your pain', and no one knows quite what to do with them. Apparently there are many in positions of power and influence who qualify for this diagnosis, but if they don't step too far out of line they are tolerated and indeed sometimes venerated for their ruthless attainment of worldly success. It gets more complicated when their lack of 'humanity' leads them to commit great crimes and their suppression is regarded as a hygienic measure in the interests of the greater good – whatever that may appear to be in the eyes of those they have damaged. Then the word 'wicked' may be employed, a word seldom given wide application.

It is most confusing and I don't know why people who believe us to be basically good do so believe. The evidence is sparse. If I live to be 103 I shall still be buttonholing passers-by and telling them about the time I went to confession and the priest said he was bothered by my lack of self-esteem. I know myself a lot better than he did. I frequently suffer remorse and don't consider it a sign of mental sickness. I will even go so far as to say I feel guilt. It is not comfortable but better than adding self-deception to the list – which would offend my sense of *amour propre*.

68. WHATEVER HAPPENED TO SEXUAL RESTRAINT?

Of all the false gods, Aphrodite and Eros are among the most alarming. I was reading some lady's account of her visit to a convent and her bafflement on discovering that the inhabitants appeared to exhibit none of the neurasthenic symptoms supposedly attendant on the celibate way of life. Since Freud – she intimated – we all believe that sex makes one, if not happy, then whole, and what precisely she thought she meant by that I do not know. Is she speaking solely of sexual intercourse, or of what are now known as 'relationships'? What does she mean by whole? Since she writes of 'one' she cannot be thinking of the old concept of the riven couple, happily reconstituted, but of the individual.

She confides that she grew up in the Sixties and believed unquestioningly that women had, for centuries, been denied their rightful pleasures and misled about the nature of their desires, which viewpoint would have come as a surprise to the *grandes horizontales* of history.

The idea that sex provides the most convenient means of procreation is increasingly frowned upon by the liberally inclined who see it, rather, as a more socially acceptable habit than smoking. Sex is revered as being of peerless importance and, at the same time, treated as a trivial diversion – at its most utilitarian in the sphere of advertising. In between the numberless ads for loans and laxatives come the ads for various things to eat, and here children are being employed to prove their usefulness: sexually aware children, which must offer great encouragement to the paedophile.

Rifling through Father's wallet, the kiddies find a picture of Baby Spice and a discussion ensues, concluding with the Benjamin of the family asking, with a knowing grin, whether Baby Spice or his mother had the nicer bottom. Another ad shows a child and her mother at the zoo, where the monkeys are behaving as monkeys will. Later, at dinner, the daughter asks what the monkeys were doing and Mother explains they were having a cuddle. Over this child's face too there then spreads a libidinous rictus, the sort of expression more usually associated with the denizens of the tap room at the Cat and Fiddle. On the radio yet another ad features a child interrogating its mother's current boyfriend on the precise nature of the kisses he exchanges with its mother and asking whether he is therefore about to become its new father.

The other day I heard a woman rejoicing that although she had been a good Catholic girl she was now bad, BAD, and wrote poetry to prove it. I don't know about her morals, but her poetry was incontestably awful. The idea was, I believe, when first promulgated, that the banishment of all sexual restraint and misguided modesty would add to the sum of human happiness and lead to the creation of ever greater art. It hasn't quite worked out like that. What we have got is Tracy Emin, Ali G and lubricious advertisements for gravy. And Aids.

69. JUDAS' KISS

The kiss of Judas is one of the worst moments in Gethsemane, for betrayal undermines all human dealings, invalidates speech, makes the ground underfoot uncertain and fills the air with fog. Since the traitor must keep for the most part in the shadows, he relies on unreality, and since his dealings are insubstantial they defy forgiveness. Judas had to hang himself. No one else would do it and there was nothing else to do, for having once accepted them, throwing down the pieces of silver came too late. Betrayal cannot be undone. The consequences are out of the hands of the traitor and are inevitable, for the traitor is, by definition, powerless.

Judas lacked even the empty potency of Pilate, who could at least wash his hands of the problem, and even those who do not see Judas as some sort of freedom fighter, who himself felt betrayed by the curious path his supposed Messiah had chosen, might feel sorry for him. He was instrumental in the tragedy in the way of a cheap tool, to be used and discarded with all the implications of that perception, loss of autonomy and dignity. The traitor's role remains insignificant in relation to the larger context. Wickeder men will use him but none will appear as contemptible as he. This is not because he acts from a position of safety: the informer is always in danger, though seldom unusually courageous, and needs help in order to become invisible as well as insubstantial, for he has no home and nobody loves him, not once he's been found out. From the humblest police snout to Sir Anthony Blunt, the traitor is loathsome. He acts in the pursuit of gain and sells his soul, a transaction close to despair, which is said to be a sin against the Holy Ghost and the one unforgivable transgression – which brings us full circle.

It is the kiss that arouses most unease in the watcher, the pretence of friendship and abuse of trust. The spy is different from the traitor, his dissembling of another nature, and he is not as horridly unnatural as the false friend, who is more abhorrent than the avowed enemy. Those scenes on TV where the good guy (or girl) insinuates himself into the confidence of the gang make one shift about on one's sofa, for betrayal, even of evil persons, implies that once there was trust, however briefly, and trust is neutral, neither good nor bad, but not to be created in order to be broken.

Out of the realm of politics or gangsterdom treachery thrives among the insecure, those who like to appear in the know. Compassion, or what looks like it, is, as often as not, curiosity. Beware of the question, 'What's wrong?' and even more of the invitation to tell the questioner all about it. The minor traitor is often motivated by social ambition and the urge to stand in reflected limelight, to let it be known by whatever means that he is close to the celebrity of the hour. Perhaps that was why Judas kissed the Lord.

70. VICE

'The lilies and languors of virtue...the roses and raptures of vice'. What, I ask myself, did the poet intend to convey by the word 'vice'? Not petty or even grand larceny, nor train robbery, forgery or cat burglary. He was thinking of boudoirs, heady potions and mind-altering substances, not boring, pedestrian crime. The prudent villain will eschew loose women, drink and drugs, particularly if he makes his livelihood from them, and is often a blameless family man, devoted to his mother and solicitous of his wife's reputation. He could be held up as a model of probity, worthy of emulation were it not for the source of wealth, and if he can contrive to keep that dark he could end up in the House of Lords.

The poet had in mind Miss Whiplash – not the career criminal, but something more picturesque – though when you think about it, languor and the pallor of the lily are more commonly associated with the consequences of excess, with the hangover and crises of the liver, than with a healthy and virtuous lifestyle. In popular literature it used to be the vicious individuals who were pock-marked, squinty-eyed and maggot-complexioned, while the good girl had roses in her cheeks.

Now, while vice might not be openly esteemed, virtue is unfashionable: moderation, modesty, chastity, frugality are regarded as character flaws, and even qualities like generosity are looked on with suspicion. Selfishness is considered the norm. There is yet another TV ad (these ads can be relied upon as an accurate indicator of social attitudes for they are made in all sincerity, from the purest of motives – the lust for money) demonstrating this said truth: a horrible old woman is cramming down a chocolate biscuit while her husband – who is clearly suffering from senile dementia – wanders back and forth calling vainly again and again for his teeth which the old cow has concealed in the fish tank.

I really must watch less TV, though the wireless can be just as irritating. There was a programme in which middle-aged women had the gall to announce that they'd been perfectly happy in their pre-comprehensive schools – one even run by nuns. The interviewer did her best, imploring them to try and remember how awful it must have been with uniforms and single-sex and rules, and surely the nuns must have been at least as cruel as Vlad the Impaler, but the ladies placidly persisted – saying it had all been very pleasant. The listener, with what the programme makers might consider a lack of discernment, would have been left with the impression that life in a convent school, where the emphasis was on virtue, could have been preferable to an apprenticeship in the massage parlours of Soho with uninhibited access to all that jolly vice.

71. MONEY

It came to me as a blinding flash of revelation. I had been listening to a discussion of the causes of crime. There were various suggestions made, such as early separation from the mother, absence of father, lack of respect for authority, peer pressure, sheer bloody-mindedness, inner city conditions, the condition of the deprived rural areas, poverty... And there it was. Obvious. Apart from crimes of passion and those committed by the potty, the cause of all crime is money. Lack of it, need for it, greed for it: whichever form the trigger takes, the result is the insatiable urge to get hold of money. From Jean Valjean, whose motives were respectable, to members of the present government who shall be nameless, thieves and con men have behaved as they do in pursuit of pelf. Those who desire drugs or trainers or international companies or blondes or Picassos or power must have the wherewithal to pay for them or consider themselves losers.

'But they that will be rich fall into temptation and a snare, and into many foolish and hurtful lusts, which drown men in destruction and perdition. For the love of money is the root of all evil: which while some coveted after, they have erred from the faith, and pierced themselves through with many sorrows', while those suddenly and unaccustomedly wealthy reveal themselves as vulgar before the sorrows get a hold. Not that it would matter much if only the innocent did not think these gilded creatures worthy of emulation and even respect, and attempt to decorate themselves in the same fashion.

Having no money at all is a liberating step on the way to enlightenment, but, it must be conceded, not having enough is an entirely different matter. The presence of the bailiffs is, if nothing else, an unwelcome distraction. The penniless and homeless can afford to look down on the rest of us from their lofty perspective, free of cares or irritations, though it helps if you live in a country with a pleasant climate and a charitable population prepared to revere your heroic frugality and give you things to eat.

Paying no taxes must, in itself, be satisfying – which brings us to yet another of the penalties consequent on the possession of money: robbers, moths and rust are a nuisance but nothing is as exquisitely annoying as watching your hard-earned money being taken by scoundrels to paper their walls with. I don't think anyone now imagines that people go into politics with any other aim than to improve their status while wasting vast sums on whatever stupid idea has presently taken hold of them. Eminent persons used to be admired for their qualities (no matter how illusory); now they are envied for their riches. But then – as St Paul also pointed out to Timothy – you can't take it with you, or rather, 'For we brought nothing into this world, and it is certain we can carry nothing out.'

72. WRECKERS

꙳ ✢ ꙳

One of my correspondents says I should do more for the Faith, or when the time comes for me to account for the way I spent my time on earth I'll find myself at a loss. This is unfair. I wrote a whole book about what the destroyers were doing to the Church and I remarked, amongst other things, on the consequences of Worlock's time as Archbishop of Liverpool. These activities brought the whole new liberal, tolerant, inclusive post-Vatican II mob screaming to my door. There is nothing more drippingly venomous than an unappreciated liberal. I detest the whole heretical, smarmy, treacherous lot of them, but what can I do without repeating myself?

A month ago in France I was talking to a perfectly – on the face of it – intelligent female who told me that the previous tenant of her house had gone to be cared for by nuns. Lucky old her, said I, adding provocatively that when I could no longer clean my own teeth I intended to follow her example. I had to wait no more than a second. But nuns are so cruel, gasped my companion, as I had known she would. On the previous Sunday I had shocked two expats, who were sniggering at the benighted natives on their way to church, by leaping from the bar stool and crying that I must rush or I'd be late for Mass. They looked at me as old China hands might have looked at a compatriot who'd announced her intention to bind her feet.

Not that the Faith in France is in any better state than it is here. The church I was making for is stripped to the bare walls and periodically adorned with awful drawings done by the local *enfants*. Should I have yet again explained that I had known nuns all my life and they had, with one or two exceptions, been perfectly charming until Vatican II when the aggressive feminist sort appeared, than with whom one would rather spend one's declining years with the wild beasts of the *forêt*?

We are in a situation where non-believers *do* believe the propaganda of the wreckers, share their ignorant contempt for the old ways and have no knowledge of, or interest in, what the wreckers like to call 'the new springtime of the Church' or 'the fruits of the Council'. The liberals who make up the larger part of the destructive movement are against authority, hierarchy, structure and discipline, and many of them don't believe in God; their multi-fruited springtime has brought about a catastrophic decline in Church attendance and vocations, while it seems that a disproportionate number of priests have turned sex fiends and their bishops have striven to protect them from exposure.

There were many ghastly mistakes made in the Sixties for which society is still paying the price, but Springtime was the most disastrous. What more can I say? Dwelling on the horror puts me into an unfit state of mind even to think about approaching the Gates of St Peter.

73. SEA OF FAITH

Sea of Faith sounds nice until you start remembering old sayings about being all at sea where worse things happen, and thinking about what the march of progress has done to the actual ones – used them like the town drain and filled them up with pollutants, drastically reduced the number of their inhabitants, built a grisly frill of holiday hotels along their margins and launched a lot of floating motels to cruise about on them, as well as tankers leaking oil, etc., etc.

I have met a few people who belong to the organization they call Sea of Faith (one was a Roman Catholic priest who believed in neither the Virgin Birth nor the Resurrection) and read and heard the outpourings of others, and I can't see the point. I can completely understand those who don't believe in God, for sitting in a certain position looking up a particular chimney I don't myself, but I fail to see why anyone should wish to be a minister of religion if he, or indeed she, does not subscribe to the tenets of same. It's rather as if I should aspire to be a Freemason or Hell's Angel. There was a Reverend on the radio only recently earnestly explaining that it was quite acceptable for Christians not to believe in anything they are told in the New Testament, or in a Creator or in anything they might find a little difficult to comprehend, while they could, if they fancied, believe in reincarnation; and, he concluded with an air of triumph, there was even a saint who described God as 'Nothing'.

How to explain that this 'Nada' is not intended in the same sense as 'nothing in the fridge'? It would be far easier to get along with the Presbyterian who was also recently on the radio claiming, by implication, that the Ancient of Days had made it perfectly clear in the Fourth Commandment that nobody, native or tourist, should drive a motor car round the Isle of Lewis on the Sabbath. You know where you are with a Wee Free.

I don't suppose those floundering about in the Sea of Faith have much interest in seeing the churches full again, and it's hard to know what they do want. I know one of them, Don

Cupitt, wishes us to perceive, in infinity, a likeness to a dough-nut, but have never been able to grasp his precise meaning. It seems an oddly comfortless doctrine. True, I have sometimes wondered whether insistence on the overwhelming goodwill of the Almighty might not be a little misplace since the evidence of this is somewhat sparse, but when the going gets really trying I would prefer to think in terms of fathers rather than doughnuts. The simplicity of the Creed veils a profundity which the 'intel-lectuals', Bible scholars and nitpickers fail to notice or to convey. I do not believe, as they apparently do, that we are all becoming more godlike as time goes by, are sharing in the work of creation and will end up omniscient. Fellow of All Souls is about the height of human attainment – acknowledgment of which truth should restore us all to a state of proper humility.

74. CEREMONIES, RITUALS

Just as a formal education serves to discourage the autodidact's promiscuous foraging in the ranks of unrelated topics in the public library, so one of the valuable functions of formal religion was to pre-empt the type of ceremony to which a friend was recently subjected – a 'christening'. 'Urghh,' commenced my friend as she strove to describe the event. 'There was this ghastly man and his ghastly daughter and her ghastly baby in this ghastly garden on the ghastly borders of ghastly Middlesex and this ghastly man read out a ghastly bit from the ghastly Bible' (my friend was exasperated beyond the capacity for measured discrimination and anyway might well have been referring to a piece from one of the newer translations, in which case the adjective was not unjust) 'and then someone said something of a Buddhist nature and someone else said something of a Hindu stamp and everyone walked round in circles patting the baby and songs were sung. *Ghastly* songs,' said my friend, shuddering.

The ancient Greeks had a ceremony called the Amphidromia wherein the father of the neonate took all his clothes off and ran round in circles with it while the friends of the family brought it presents of octopuses, but my friend seems not to have noticed the child's father in the scene depicted. Maybe he was drinking in the shrubbery. Admittedly even Christian christenings are not what they were, although I did attend one just the other day where the vicar was addressed as Father and well out-Catholicked the Romans in his adherence to tradition, but on the whole no one likes to hear mention of the Devil and all his works because that isn't a very nice thing to imply about the little baby, as surely it is basically good and enters the world free of sin – a view which renders Christ and His mission entirely redundant.

The funeral service has long been bowdlerized, eviscerated and smothered in syrup because bodily corruption is a horrid thing to mention at an interment and might upset the bereaved, who prefer to 'celebrate the life' of the deceased. Spirituality, which accepts the reality of pain and loss and unendurable grief, has been superseded by sentimentality, which seeks to ameliorate such negative emotions and obscure them in soap-suds.

A friend of a friend (this is not an urban myth) went to one of those newly fashionable weddings where the principals subject each other to speeches of their own devising. She tried desperately to think of something else as the sweat of embarrassment ran in rivulets down her back, and then they each lit a candle – so there were two – and with these they lit another – so there was one. Oh God.

They are now proposing a form of ceremony to mark divorce, which might be quite refreshing if a spark of honest emotion was permitted to appear. 'Wilt thou do all that thou canst to screw every bean out of this person?' 'I will.'

75. CROSS

A correspondent asks why I'm so cross. Because everything is so annoying, I suppose. Of course one gets cross. Wherever one goes one gets cross. Trains, planes, supermarkets, streets, country lanes where one suddenly encounters bungalows with names and fancy walls that have sprung up overnight, pubs where they've ripped out the interior, churches (same treatment), everywhere from the homogenized inner cities to the neglected countryside is the very stuff of crossness.

Some suggest trying Christian forbearance, but that can easily be mistaken for craven passivity. Christ Himself was not always notable for His patience. Those oleaginous persons who go about oozing sweetness and light in what they consider a Christ-like fashion are among the most annoying of all. Some persist in attempting to touch you and looking into your eyes and smiling... The very word 'Christian' shows signs of going the way of the Union Jack, of losing its original significance and becoming the badge of the limp and wimpy, as the flag became the symbol of the skinhead.

And then there is the irritation caused by the nun-bashers: endless whining about the Marquis de Sade-like sisters who ruined their childhoods and bent their self-esteem all out of shape. I heard a woman describing what a naughty little thing she'd been and how, at her confirmation, she had elected to add Mary Magdalen to her name and how the nuns had drawn in their breath and the bishop had blushed scarlet and wasn't that daring and amusing and original – to which one can only respond that if the convent did not already harbour a Sister Mary Magdalen then it was unusual, for this friend of Our Lord was accorded great affection and respect when I was a child and in the company of nuns. Why, one wonders, did the lady bother to invent this tale? Perhaps to make herself more interesting. Now I come to think of it, nuns were always more interesting than lay females, skilled in exegesis and not given to asking where you bought your lipstick or swooning over Frank Sinatra.

I used to get cross even then when I saw my schoolmates swooning over Frank Sinatra: he looked spivvish and had a prominent Adam's apple.

I know how not to be cross: all one has to do is throw out the TV and wireless, find some substitute for newspaper with which to light the fire, and avoid company. The eremitic option is seductive and attainable and you can spend your days addressing yourself to God. The only problem is that if he hasn't actually called you to this way of life, you could end up talking to yourself and getting madder and madder. All I know is that there is no virtue in the placid acceptance of life's more egregious errors and failures, and while Job is a more edifying character than Jeremiah he is harder to emulate.

76. ANNOYING ATHEISTS

Atheism is not at present fashionable, taking second place to a light syrup of New Age 'Thinking'. It makes an appearance in every generation, meeting with varying degrees of acceptance whilst not varying much in its nature. The cordiality of the atheist's dislike of God is often far greater than the ardour of the believer – which is usually sadly lukewarm. The sentiment, 'I don't believe in Him but I hate Him', is surprisingly common in atheistic attitudes. Some atheists are that way because they can't help it and have never been touched by doubt, but many have an axe to grind. These are the argumentative sort who find belief in God as irritating as the fashion-conscious find, say, the Duchess of York or the wife of the Prime Minister. 'You're supposed to be an intelligent person,' they say. 'How can you believe all that tosh/wear that hat with those shoes?'

This is where the pious expectation that *talking* will resolve all differences falls down. Both parties may talk until they're blue in the face but neither will gain an inch of ground. It would be easier for the non-believer, who after all, has logic, reason and common sense on his side, if the believer believed only because he had been told and taught to, but if the believer has encountered God he can no sooner deny it than profess never to have met his mother. The atheist will insist that the encounter is illusory – the result of neurosis, wish-fulfilment, drink, drugs, clinical insanity or a wish to appear more virtuous, wiser, more profound than the rest.

The most infuriating manifestation of all is the appearance of serenity. Unless this tranquillity is earned by a courageous response to adversity and is reinforced by an accompanying wit and knowledge of the world, then it quite properly brings out the worst in all of us. Or rather, most of us: some people are more easily conned than others, and fall in behind frightful charlatans with smooth countenances and enormous bank balances.

Christianity is even less fashionable than atheism – which is largely the fault of the leadership, who think it would go down better if it were a bit more like atheism, sensible stuff with an appeal to the reasonable man, or, on the other hand, jolly and unthreatening with an appeal to the simple-minded – a term which they appear to believe sums up most of us. It was my huband who insisted on describing a religious fanatic as one who believes in God, and I see what he meant. Fire and fervour are still perceived as un-British. Lucy Lethbridge and Selina O'Grady have compiled a book, *A Deep but Dazzling Darkness* (Darton, Longman & Todd), consisting of quotes from people who have met God, and I don't suppose it will sell like Beckham's memoirs. It will, however, annoy any atheist who happens upon it because God keeps making an appearance in its pages, as unlikely yet as undeniable as a celebrity at a parish garden party. Now you see him, now you don't – but He is certainly among those present.

77. REPENTANCE

The death of Myra Hindley caused many people to express their opinions of her. Nothing new was said, as they repeated what they had always thought, that she was either damned or saved and no two ways about it. Some said, good, she's gone to hell and serve her right, while others explained that they'd met her and she was really awfully nice. One or two who had also met her said she wasn't, but that view does not sound so original or put the viewer in the position of sage and seer, able to discern, through the mire, the underlying worth of even the most reviled human being. One man suggested that she merely exemplified to an unfortunate degree the darkness inherent in all of us, to which one can only respond in the popular phrase – *Excuse me...* Humility is all very well but there is no virtue in pretending to a viciousness we do not possess. I'm sure most of us could kill if the need arose, but few of us would torture a child to death, and the hint that we all harbour perverse inclinations and are prevented from indulging them only by a hypocritical lack of honesty and the crippling constraints of society is, to say the least, impertinent.

It was said that Hindley was truly repentant, but one is inclined to agree with those who claim that if this had been the case, she would not have sought release from prison and would have revealed the whereabouts of the graves of her victims.

There appears to be a pervasive sense in the air around the *bien pensant* that even the most deep-dyed villains improve with time, as though remorse were somehow inevitable and not dependent on the examination of conscience or the recognition of the error of their ways, and that they become fit for polite society after a given period of incarceration, having 'paid their debt' to the above. This is understandable in the purveyors of religion, since repentance is part of their stock-in-trade and if they doubted its existence they would lose their *raison d'être*, but in everyone else it seems irrational. Where is the evidence? I have a friend who drinks with a number of ex-bank robbers whom the starry-eyed might describe as 'reformed': that is, they no longer rob banks, though not because they have thought better of it. They have all retained a genteel sufficiency enabling them to live comfortably, and they are all, to be frank, past it – old and not very well. None of them evinces remorse. Robbing banks was what they did. They got locked up for it and now they're out. End of story. The two murderers I know (there may be others but these got caught) are what is known as 'in denial', refusing to entertain any thoughts of guilt or shame and insisting on seeing themselves as unlucky.

On the other hand, I know people who suffer agonies because they were inadvertently short with the girl at the checkout, or left the cat outside overnight. The greater the sin, the less the remorse.

78. UNCONDITIONAL LOVE

With the decline of the Christian religion, some of its followers have taken to spin, striving to rebrand and repackage it and make it attractive to the consumer. In furtherance of this aim they have given the CEO a makeover. They still call him God but make frequent reference to his unconditional love. The word 'unconditional' is, on the evidence, inaccurate.

Opening the Bible at random, although admittedly roughly in the area where one knows the more savage bits to lie, one finds in Zechariah the lines following the sighting of the 'flying roll'. 'This is the curse that goeth forth over the face of the whole earth,' declares the Lord of Hosts, and goes on to explain that 'it shall enter into the house of the thief and of him that sweareth falsely by his name' and 'consume it with the timber thereof and the stones thereof'.

Turning back to Ezekiel, one finds the Lord in a terrible temper. 'I will also destroy the idols and I will cause their images to cease out of Noph... and I will put a fear in the land of Egypt. And I will make Pathros desolate, and will set fire in Zoan, and will execute judgments in No. And I will pour my fury upon Sin, the strength of Egypt...' And so on, with threats of great pain and rendings asunder and fire and daily distresses and fallings by the sword and captivity and God knows what (as it were) – pages and pages of talk of blood, fire, terror, graves, abominations, the horrible fate of the uncircumcised, hell, the pit, shame, and not one squeak of unconditional love.

So I turn to the New Testament and find myself in the Gospel according to Matthew with the warning to child abusers: 'But whoso shall offend one of these little ones which believe in me [note the proviso] it were better for him that a millstone were hanged about his neck, and that he were drowned in the depth of the sea'. That part goes on with talk of woe and offences and cutting off of offending hands and feet and plucking out of eyes. It is certainly mellower than the Old Testament, but 'unconditional' is still not the *mot juste*. There follows the parable about forgiveness which has given rise to a degree of unfounded complacency amongst malefactors as they neglect to understand that the forgiveness of God is conditional. 'And his lord was wroth and delivered him to the tormentors, till he should pay all that was due unto him. So likewise shall my heavenly Father do also unto you, if ye from your hearts forgive not every one his brother their trespass.'

Such rigour must seem shocking in an atmosphere where forgiveness is redundant since our genes are responsible for our behaviour, and blame is aimed mainly at those who, the feeling is, should have foreseen the future and prevented things from happening: accidents, corruption, war, plague. We do not like authority but we believe someone should be in charge. I can imagine God gnashing the holy teeth, and one can't really blame him.

79. LIFE IS WEIRD ENOUGH

I read that Philip Pullman hates C. S. Lewis. I'm not mad about him either, having, in my youth, preferred the *William* books to tales of Narnia, but I couldn't be bothered to hate him. Nor could I, in my youth, be bothered with works of fantasy. I still can't, come to think of it – life is weird enough already, and as for the wardrobes, I have problems of my own just walking into, let alone through them. In the summer I had several battles with a bat which considered it had right of tenure alongside the Jean Muir and the charity shop discoveries, and apart from that, most of the garments crammed in there appear to have been designed for a person of a different shape. Besides, I always thought a wardrobe, with its mothballs and fluff, an ill-considered choice of departure point for other worlds.

Enough of all this lit crit. It seems that Mr Pullman really hates Christianity. He reminds one of the school bully who is too prudent to pick on the big kids who fight back but regularly beats up the non-combatant – the Church Militant having long packed up its tents and even its bivouacs. The Church now behaves like the school patsy, placating, simpering, eager not to annoy, rolling over with its paws in the air. A sorry spectacle.

In the rush to people-please, someone has attempted yet again to make the Bible more accessible. A man on the wireless recently revealed that Jesus said to his disciples something on the lines of, 'Don't bother about all those fish, soon you'll be catching people,' which sounds as though it should be addressed to the Old Bill rather than the missionary. For all the cloth-eared to whom this sort of thing appeals there must be thousands who would prefer the phrase 'fishers of men'. Is ugliness more politically correct, or is it that we are considered too stupid to appreciate beauty?

Then I saw a programme about Liverpool Cathedral, the RC one, in which it was explained that the place was designed so that no one should feel excluded from the proceedings. Young and old, rich and poor, saint and sinner alike could sit in a circle and join in and no one need sit at the back. It may come as a surprise, but all the above were once expected – nay, required – to turn up, and if they didn't like sitting at the back all they had to do was arrive earlier and sit at the front. Anyway, some people preferred sitting at the back, reflecting, as the drama of the Mass proceeded and the priest did what he was ordained to do. They felt no need to be 'empowered' to take a more active role. If they couldn't follow what was going on they had merely to consult the stage directions in the Missal, and if the Latin was beyond them there was the English translation alongside. Being compelled to straighten up and pay attention strikes me as more impertinently bossy than being compelled merely to be there. The implication again is that we are too dumb to be left to our own devices and must have the pages turned for us.

80. GHOST

I am not a great admirer of children's art, music or poetry: it seems self-evident that with a bit more experience and a lot of practice they are bound to get better at it and, on the whole, I do not enjoy their childish prattle, their passion for repetition or who's-there jokes. It takes some years before they can mean to be funny and get it right, and when they are unintentionally funny it seems discourteous to laugh at them. And like most people I run a mile from those who show signs of being about to tell you what their grandchildren said at breakfast. So I've given you fair warning.

Now picture the scene: it is morning and my daughter is applying her make-up by the light of an upper window, her four-year-old son beside her. He speaks: 'Who's that man, Mummy?' 'What man?' asks his mother, squinting through the application of mascara. 'That one', says the child impatiently, pointing at the gate to a field. After a moment there is a call from my daughter: 'Mum, come here. Isaac's seeing a ghost'. I've never seen one, although I've heard them, so I hasten upstairs and kneel by the window. I can't see anything so I ask what the man is wearing. 'Brown coat, green hat', says the child. 'Can you see his face?' I enquire. 'Yes', he says. 'Nice face?' I ask. 'No', says the child matter-of-factly. 'He's dead'.

We don't know how he knows what *dead* is; his parents have not read to him from *The Water Babies* or any of that Victorian crypt literature for tots, he has not yet been obliged to conduct a funeral service for a deceased pet, on *Tom and Jerry*, etc., nothing stays dead even though destroyed, and he has not seen that film about the clairvoyant little boy. And he is too young for dissimulation. A friend reminds me that somebody we knew years ago used to hold that people under the age of five could discern the dead in a crowded street; she used to take her grandson walking round Hampstead dead-spotting.

Isaac is a religious child. I can't say he believes in God because that implies faith and he doesn't need it, being on intimate terms with the Almighty. A newborn baby lies in its cot, gazing upwards as babies will. 'I wonder what he's looking at,' muse the parents. 'God, of course,' says Isaac with a touch of contempt for their lack of perception. But his relationship with God has no obvious connection with his awareness of death. It may be that people who have not been born for very long are more sanguine about not being here, and the veil for them is thinner. Once they were not and one day they will not be. So what? A year later Isaac is still cool about death. Having drawn a picture of a smiling figure with a decided list to port he observes, 'I think this person's dyin''. 'No, no,' I cry brightly. 'It looks quite happy.' 'It's happy it's dyin',' says the child, growing exasperated. 'It doesn't want to see no one.'

81. MERCIFUL RELEASE

They (the people who take it upon themselves to say this sort of thing) tell us that our life expectancy is lengthening significantly, which comes with the suspicion that society will be hard put to it to sustain a large elderly population. They give the impression that it is thoughtless of people to persist in living on when they can no longer be of use and are merely a drain on resources. The young and able-bodied, they seem to hint, should be free to pursue happiness and wealth and not be constrained to minister to the ailing and the old.

The more utilitarianly minded increasingly attempt to make the concept of euthanasia respectable, others insist on the sanctity of life, while on the wilder shores of science people are circling round the idea of physical immortality, suggesting that if we find the reason why ageing occurs, then we can do something about it. The fact that we just get older with the passage of time doesn't satisfy them; there must, they say, be something else we should eat, some gene we could modify, *something*. They begin by saying that we could live cheerful, vigorous lives without being a nuisance until the age of 127 or more, but I suspect that they're thinking *forever*. They clearly cannot mean that *everyone* should live forever – which is alarming, for who is to decide?

But another trouble here is that the mere fact of them wanting to be around indefinitely reveals them as people with a lack of imagination. There surely would come a moment when they would have to confront the awful boredom of things, the realization that they'd done everything before, and before that. There would be no real future, only an endless past, and all the more intelligent and amusing people would, consciously or not, have availed themselves of the fatal possibilities afforded by accident.

What are the elderly to do as they see succeeding generations making an even worse pig's ear of everything than they did themselves? Their criticism is not welcome, their advice is disregarded, and everywhere they go their very appearance reminds the young and lively that Death is waiting in the wings.

The only answer lies in an alteration in our attitude to this inescapable fact. There have always been people – and on the whole they have been religious people – who take the serene approach to the inevitable, anticipating an improvement in their circumstances when the final moment has come and gone. I don't suggest that we should go round in our dotage smirking smugly as the escape date grows closer, but we could bear in mind the old cliché about the merciful release and agree to go quietly. If you believe the promises of God, then death beats winning the pools in terms of reward and all-round satisfaction. Resignation is unfashionable in an age when choice is regarded as a human right, but this is a case where there's no point in arguing.

82. VICE AND VIRTUE

The idea that vice is attractive is being used by the advertising industry at present to persuade us to eat ice-cream. The campaign is working its way through the Seven Deadly Sins, when you would have thought a simple appeal to Gluttony would have sufficed. A group of impossibly glamorous females is deployed to illustrate the message. Vice-cream, perhaps.

Admittedly, if the advertising agencies must concern themselves with abstruse theological considerations, the Seven Virtues could not be considered a *sine qua non* in commerce. The supernatural three might motivate those inclined towards Faith, Hope and Charity to contribute to Oxfam, the RSPCA, etc., but of the four Cardinal Virtues (Prudence, Justice, Fortitude and Temperance) only the first might prove compelling in the sale, for instance, of reliable cars, loo rolls, insurance policies and implements to prevent emulsion paint from getting on the door frames and light fittings. Advertising companies must regard the last three Virtues with abhorrence.

In the real world, however, the Seven Virtues are undeniably desirable, not to say utilitarian. Faith and Hope help keep you cheerful, Charity helps cheer up the other person, while adherence to the last four will, DV, keep you out of prison. If A, whom you had thought as honest as the day is long, makes off with your Rolex, you do not thereby feel warmer towards him. If B, whom you had considered a loyal soul, turns out to be a treacherous old hyena, you do not immediately think her more interesting. If C is pointed out to you in the pub as a suspected serial murderer, you do not hasten to make his acquaintance. Certainly we must be charitable and not judge (lest we, etc.) but that is where Prudence comes into it. Temperance, too, is useful in these circumstances, since even the well-disposed drunk so quickly loses the capacity to evaluate a situation clearly and sensibly, making rash promises and signing cheques, which necessitates ringing the bank the minute it opens in the morning in order to cancel them. We could all do with more Justice, and Fortitude is invaluable in the quotidian struggle to keep in place the 'painted veil which those who live call life' – a line which the advertisers could adopt as their own, now I come to think of it.

The preference for vice over virtue is the consequence of Original Sin, and if that idea makes you scream, ask someone who knows – where lie the survival advantages in Sloth, Wrath, Envy, Pride, Gluttony, Lust and Avarice? Briefly, these, taken one by one, cause people to lose their jobs, have fits of road-rage, chew the counterpane in spite, fall over, grow obese, get divorced, and end up in court. Oddly enough, these are not the polar opposites of the Virtues, or the sins which most annoy God (that distinction belongs to Despair), but they do conspire to make life foul, even if they help sell ice-cream.

83. SAINTS

When the Pope decided to canonize the latest batch of saints, I heard someone bleating tremulously that the Church did not canonize ordinary women but tended to honour queens and nuns. I cannot, offhand, think of all that many sainted queens, but am not startled to hear that nuns figure largely on the list. It is to be expected, rather than wondered at, that some should excel in their chosen way of life, especially if they start young.

Married ladies and career women do not have the same opportunity or encouragement to attain the heights of sanctity, and it must be admitted that saints can be a little tiresome under ordinary circumstances, and not the kind of person you really want around the house or in the office.

The saint, like it or not, has a special relationship with God, and it takes more work than other more mundane relationships which, God knows, can be difficult enough.

He, or, for present purposes, she, does not feel free to claim indulgence and make excuses for a lack of zeal in the way that the rest of us do. She is always on duty, always aware of her goal and alert to the wiles of the Evil One. Yes, I know it sounds quaint, but that's the point. Few people see it that way and restrict themselves to paying their taxes and not kicking the cat. This is commendable but unlikely to lead to a ceremony at St Peter's. Elitism is frowned upon, but not all of us can make it to the boardroom or the Centre Court at Wimbledon. Not all of us want to, not possessing the drive.

I like nuns – the old sort, that is, not the new, feminist mob. I like convents: the quiet, the sense of order and peace, the absence of untidiness and rush, the smell of incense and beeswax and occasional wafts of cabbage from the kitchens. And nuns are often very funny, a sense of humour being useful when it comes to dealing with the Almighty, not to mention living in Community. They are rarely found screeching with rage or throwing things or complaining bitterly because their nearest and dearest are paying them insufficient attention. It seems that as more and more families split asunder, expectations rise rather than sink to a realistic level.

Nuns support, but do not rely on, each other for psychological and spiritual fulfilment. The saints (male and female) who founded the great Orders and Communities were masters of psychology and acutely aware of what would and would not lead to harmonious conditions between the walls: they could teach the gurus of today a thing or two. God first, others second, self third is a good recipe for life and could result, if widely applied, in an increase in contented people even if not a sudden surge in the number of saints. Though, come to think of it, it might, as long as they make allowances for the shortcomings of the rest of us, not imposing their own standards.

84. THE TALKING CURE

❧ ✿ ❧

There is a fixed idea that talk is a good thing, and a nice chat will go a long way towards settling disputes. I cannot imagine why so many people subscribe to this notion. As far as I'm aware, every discussion of any knotty topic ends with the participants more firmly entrenched than before in their various positions and even less kindly inclined to the other side. If they part without bloodshed they will go over the event in their minds, tortured by itchy *esprit d'escalier*-type thoughts, vowing that next time Bloggs says that stupid thing, they will respond by handing him a smack in the mouth.

How often do we feel the temptation to take a swing at the TV with the poker or fling the radio from a high window as we hear our leaders gabbling evasions, blaming the Opposition for the state we're in, or simply lying? Pipe down, we hear ourselves scream. Do something useful, get a job, *go away*. They doubtless thought that we would appreciate them more if we were enabled to listen to or watch them engaged in 'debate', as they describe the mix of boasting and invective that characterizes the Lower Chamber, but they were mistaken. The impression gained is not one of civilized discourse but of 'Yah boo sucks'.

I do not know any people who have had their problems solved by the 'Talking Cure': it has often kept them off the streets but that was usually because they were too self-involved to go out and anyway they couldn't afford it once they'd paid the analyst. People in 'relationships' are earnestly advised to talk over their problems, and the next thing is the neighbours are calling the police. There have been times and places where Muslim, Jew and Christian have got along without undue stress, exchanging harmless pleasantries, buying and selling, even lending umbrellas or a cup of sugar in emergencies, but you can be sure they seldom sat down together to elaborate on their differences.

The Church of England doddled along for years with homosexual clergy, but it was only when they decided to talk it over and come out into the open that the whole edifice showed signs of falling apart; standing around in the open, after all, is just asking to be picked off. Where do they think talking will get them when it will only encourage the opposing factions to state more explicitly their reasons for or against? It might well get highly unsavoury.

It is lying that leads to despair but it must be admitted that telling the truth can lead to trouble: 'You look like hell without a brassière, dear.' I'm not suggesting that none of us should ever say anything, merely that our reverence for talk is misplaced. 'The tongue holds the key to life and death' (*Proverbs* 18:21), and the founders of the great Orders sensibly insisted that for most of the time silence should prevail in the cloisters. As the Lord put it, 'Be still and know that I am God.' Or to put it another way, 'Shut up.'

85. RELIGION AND SEX

Some years ago we gave a lunch party for a Professor of Classics: he was particularly expert on the subject of Ancient Greek sexuality and while downing the olives and anchovies – a course once known as the 'provocatives' – told us that the word 'homosexuality' was a misnomer, that the Greeks did not regard it as an alternative to heterosexuality and that the word 'sex' could properly be used only in the context of procreation; the people who had once been referred to as 'inverts' were being misrepresented and whatever they were doing it wasn't sex as such, since it was only males and females who did that. And he ate another anchovy, seemingly unaware that a fellow guest was a little disturbed by this view and had fallen silent.

I got the impression that he found the proposition demeaning. It is getting fashionable no longer to insist on the 'beauty of sex' but to suggest that not only sodomy but all genital acts are disgusting and so what? Sex is cheap and cheerful and it's hopelessly out of date to harp on about its utilitarian and procreative aspects.

I have since thought about the vexed question of religion and sex and wondered what the much-vaunted 'goddess' would have made of homosexuality. She is still approved of and sought after by New Agers and the nuttier feminist element in the Church, who insist that she was in overall charge until patriarchy came along and spiked the fun which, one gathers, was untrammelled by tiresome rules and inhibitions. Judaeo-Christianity, they hold, put a damper on unconfined joy and made everyone miserable.

The trouble with this is that everything we know about goddess cults suggests that their prime concern was with fruitfulness – an abundance of crops, animals, people – and while the various goddesses welcomed human sacrifice they abhorred sterility. Therefore, one imagines, they would have frowned upon wasteful genital activity, regarding it with more disapproval than do even the most fervent evangelicals of today. The personification of Nature would presumably have been more virulently opposed to homosexuality than the most orthodox rabbi, priest or mullah, whose instinctive revulsion, backed up by biblical and other observations on the 'sin crying out to heaven for vengeance', is, in the main, somewhat constrained by reason and the forces of liberalism and prudence.

The merciless Earth Mother, the fertility goddess, far from being benevolent and inclusive, is no more tolerant of the unfit and the unproductive than was Ayn Rand and nothing like as understanding as the Archbishop of Canterbury, and we should thank Heaven that she does not hold universal sway. Like it or not, reason, tolerance and a fairly widespread disinclination to eliminate those with whom we do not agree are the results of centuries of Christendom. There have been appalling lapses where the message of Christ has been disregarded but a return to pagan values would be ill advised.

86. FACTS OF LIFE

'Well, you see,' he said, 'of course you know I *believe* you, dearest, but excuse me, excuse me, I do *not* think it is true.' So spoke the son of Frances Hodgson Burnett (immortalized as Little Lord Fauntleroy) when he was four and 'his mama was endeavouring to explain some interesting point in connection with the structure of his small, plump body'. One of my friends met a similar response from her five-year-old son when she had explained to him the purpose of a condom found abandoned on the beach. 'Yes, Mum,' he said with weary impatience, 'but what's it *really* for?'

What is noteworthy about these anecdotes is the evident truth that small children are not ready to assimilate them. Now it seems that Channel 4 has produced a graphic video designed to teach five-year-olds the aforementioned facts of life, and 'horrified mothers' have condemned it as virtually pornographic.

Some years ago a prominent advocate of homosexual rights published a letter in a national daily paper claiming that he knew several people who had encountered paedophiles in their early years and gained nothing but joy from the experience. Paedophiles themselves make this claim and would doubtless feel vindicated if a wide swathe of society were to agree that tots should take a rest from laboriously inscribing 'the cat sat on the mat' to familiarize themselves with the nomenclature and function of all body parts in preparation for further instruction on 'masturbation, gay and lesbian relationships and the purpose [here we go again] of condoms', before proceeding to the next lesson – whereupon they will all get straight As, go to college and holiday on a Greek island, getting hopelessly inebriated and contracting venereal disease.

The liberals' solution, when they see a policy failing, is not to abandon but intensify it, and it is the responsibility of the victims of the liberal to clear their heads and shake themselves free of the vaporous atmosphere. Having seen a TV programme featuring our young on their holidays abroad, I looked up the words of a

Jesuit written in 1913: 'Eliminate from your lectures the details of sex hygiene, cast aside textbook and chart. Train your children's character, teach them that purity is noble and possible, that vice is vile and carries with it punishment... teach them that their bodies are vessels of an immortal soul made in the image and likeness of God...teach them reserve, modesty in manner and dress...'

You can laugh but, boiled down, what the good priest was saying was: do not destroy your liver and lights with prodigious quantities of alcohol, nor fornicate with five drunken strangers before closing time, nor wave your chest and bottom at the startled locals, and so, in the final analysis, do not be a prat. Leaving aside for the moment the immortal soul, the all too mortal carcass cannot cope with that degree of self-inflicted punishment.

87. SUPERIORITY

That regrettable bunch, the *unco guid*, have altered their *modus operandi* and moved about a bit; the original sort, who displayed their superiority by disapproving of the rest of us, are fewer in number and their successors aim for the same result by disapproving of nobody except those who disapprove of somebody else. We must not be judgemental, they say, smiling all over their faces and contriving simultaneously to wag their fingers, pat themselves on the back and hug sinners.

There are still some of us who were brought up to be polite, a practice now cast aside in favour of political correctness – a doctrine which assumes that only its adherents know how to behave – and while I'm not sure what is involved in the sucking of eggs, I resent being lectured on deportment. A chap, Thinking for the Day, told us on the radio that he had once 'had the nerve' to deplore racism in front of an audience wistful for the era of apartheid, and seemed unaware that he was not as unusual or shiningly brave as he supposed. In my closest group of family and friends there is a considerable degree of mixed-race marriage and none of the members find it remarkable, acclaim and criticism being equally inapplicable. The hateful will always be with us, but there is nothing to be gained by assuming that the majority secretly share their views. I saw a Boer on TV insisting that he had done nothing out of the way in beating a black worker and proceeding to jump on him ('it's the only way they learn'), but he knew no better.

He went on to say that if a white man claimed to love a black, or vice versa, he was a liar. I don't know what the traditional *unco guid* would make of him, and suspect he might have been one of them, but while any true Christian would certainly find him a worthy object of disapproval, the *unco guid* in another sphere would agree with his latter statement. Which is breathtakingly extraordinary. The social services some years ago held that white people were incapable of truly loving a black child and should not be permitted to adopt one. I've been told it still is policy, but they've gone somewhat quiet. Roy Kerridge is brilliant on this matter and his book, *Subjects of the Queen*, should be required reading across the land. It is savage and true and cool, in the sense of measured, without a hint of hypocrisy.

For an illustration of the *unco guid* in action one could do worse than watch reruns of *Quincy* on TV. The hero goes round roaring about things that anyone with half a brain could tell him were obvious injustices. If the self-righteous were only to forgo the opportunity to disport themselves on the moral high ground and instead encourage the development of simple human common sense in those they seek to influence, it would go a long way towards dispelling prejudice, and we might hate them less if they would just shut up trying to persuade us that we all hate each other.

88. MOTHER TERESA AND CHRISTOPHER HITCHENS

Some years ago I was asked to review a book by Christopher Hitchens called *The Missionary Position*. It was all about Mother Teresa, towards whom he seemed to feel a deep personal antipathy. Just before her beatification he turned up on the radio with his feelings clearly unmodified by the passage of time. He hates her. She was obviously not the sort of female to whom he is accustomed, but this does not seem sufficient reason for the force of his passion. Is it because he hates the Catholic Church? He writes that, 'In 1973 it was Prince Philip's turn to make an emotional demonstration, which he did while presenting the Templeton Prize for the "promotion of faith in the world". In the presence of his wife, who holds the title of Defender of the Faith against all the works of Rome and who heads a family which is barred from making a marriage to a Roman Catholic, the royal consort handed over £34,000.' I don't think Mr Hitchens can know that the title was bestowed by the Pope on Henry VIII before the monarch – who had the unparalleled chutzpah to hang on to it – was led astray by lust and ambition.

He, that is, Mr Hitchens, read that on another occasion 'the prize winner herself had come to the Vatican on the city bus, and was wearing her Indian sari, worth about $1'. 'If true', says Mr Hitchens, 'this was ostentatious of her'. Should she have arrived in a stretch limo or what? As he complains that she spoke to rich and nasty people in order to make them give her money for some dark purpose of her own, it is hard to follow his thought processes. In his eyes she could do nothing right.

He goes on to mention a documentary on her work that he and others made called *Hell's Angel*: 'Her response was to say that she "forgave" us for making it'. And here Mr Hitchens displays ignorance of the tenets of Christianity. He says that was odd since he had not sought her forgiveness, and it was odder still if you were inclined to ask 'by what right she assumes the power to forgive.' The only petition in the Lord's Prayer that carries a condition is the petition for forgiveness: 'Forgive us our trespasses as we forgive those who trespass against us'; and as Christ said to Peter, who had asked how oft he should forgive his brother: 'I say not unto thee, until seven times seven, but until seventy times seven.' Mother Teresa was following orders, and you would have thought that anyone of Mr Hitchen's age who had passed through the school system might have some glimmering of awareness of these well-known quotations. The blurb on his book says, as blurbs will, that he is 'One of today's most devastating polemicists.' But he does not sound very well educated and his reaction to Mother Teresa makes him seem slightly unhinged. Goodness in others is perceived by some individuals as an affront and we should understand and forgive them, not only because it is incumbent on us, but because we know – God forgive us – that it will annoy the hell out of them.

89. BARK, BARK

A child asks: when a dog barks, does he know what he is saying? This is obviously one of those profound questions bristling with philosophical, anthropomorphic and linguistic connotations and impossible to answer unless you go for the easy option and explain that the dog is probably indicating that if you do not heed its bark it will bite you. The child will throw in questions like this when he's been instructed to shut up about the emperor's new clothes or warned not to enquire once more about how far it is to the destination and told to play quietly. He will smart at the unfairness of it, for the adults around him will undoubtedly be remarking on the vacuous nature of political utterances, wondering whether the speaker has any idea what he's talking about and concluding that whether he does or not, he is a stranger to what is generally accepted as truth. Bark, bark, bark.

The latest remarks to be overheard in public places throughout the country are: 1) Anyone with an ounce of sense would encourage their young to train as plumbers, electricians or carpenters, etc., because doctors, teachers, nurses, etc., are subjected to bureaucracy from above, abuse from below and won't be able to survive on their pensions, while all those degrees in media studies, etc., have about the same status as street litter; 2) With the rise in house prices everyone will now have to pay death duties and, having been taxed all their lives, will now be taxed again, post mortem; 3) Who cares what Prince Charles gets up to – or conversely, Prince Charles is a total twerp; 4) All politicians are liars.

Nothing new in that last. What is new and interesting is the popular response to the lies. I remember when people were gullible, many of them subscribing to the various ideologies being peddled and sharing misty-eyed visions of the utopian future upon which politicians have always relied in order to keep themselves afloat since they are such rubbish at sorting out the present. There was a time when people in the public bar could follow a political argument, understand and even believe a ministerial statement, but those days are gone. You only have to hear a person on the radio addressing another by his given name to know he is lying through his teeth. 'Well, John ...' begins the politician, and listeners everywhere emit hysterical screams and go on to kick the cat or drive dangerously. The Devil has always kept lies in the top of his tool kit – cast a few around and the resultant confusion does his work for him, especially if he throws in a lot of words too. Babel.

The other thing people are saying is that if any politician would tell the truth, admit to errors and not blame the previous government, then, as long as he kept it concise, even if he confessed to eating his grandma they would vote for him. How comforting to reflect that the second person of the Trinity is not a prepared statement or a soundbite but The Word. Just the one.

90. THUMBING THEIR NOSES

It is sometimes difficult to distinguish between sheer stupidity and bone-headed insensitivity. For instance, what are we to make of a TV advertisement which appeared in Advent portraying a woman on a stage yelping in the throes of childbirth, surrounded by a medical team and the attendant paraphernalia, encouraged by cries of 'Come on, Mary' and viewed by an audience? Someone asks whether Mr Kipling has ever previously produced a Nativity play and the vicar mumbles through a mouthful that he doesn't know, but he – i.e. Mr Kipling – does make exceedingly good cakes. There then occur the words: 'It's a girl.'

I expect the people who perpetrated the ad were pleased as Punch with this witticism. Either they were too stupid to know that it would cause offence to Christians or they didn't care. I am certain that none of them was familiar with the idea that because Mary was conceived free of Original Sin it is probable that she was spared the pains of childbirth. And I am even more certain that none of them could differentiate between the Immaculate Conception and the Virgin Birth. It is charitable to infer that they acted from ignorance, for if not, then their nasty little performance verges on the wicked, grossly disrespectful if not blasphemous and, whatever the reasons, mind-numbingly silly.

The intellectually uncertain have always found release from a sense of inferiority by being naughty, demonstrating their freedom from the constraints of thought by thumbing their noses at what they cannot understand, and since other religions are openly impatient of insult, they vent their spite and envy on Christianity, knowing that they are unlikely to get blown up as a result. Nor do the politically correct concern themselves with attacks on Christ. They save their displeasure for people like the prison officer who, having 'thrown a set of keys down a chute with undue force… explained his action by saying that he had imagined "a photo of Osama bin Laden at the bottom".' He was sacked.

Too many Church leaders are yellow-bellied sycophants, more concerned with appearing fashionably liberal than defending whatever remnants of belief they may retain. It is largely left to the laity, who too often feel impotent and marginalized, to express their outrage. I can picture certain bishops giggling weakly at the advertisement, and here's what I hope. I hope they have Mr Kipling cakes at the Episcopal tea party and I hope they choke. See what happens when the shepherds abandon their responsibilities: the sheep break out of the pasture and behave badly, in the way that the vigilante takes over when the law fails. I shall have to do penance for uncharitable thoughts and for being a bad sheep and I resent it. Whatever the worst are full of, it does not resemble passionate intensity, but the best, whoever and wherever they are, certainly lack all conviction.